POKER, FROM HOBBY TO BUSINESS

2nd Edition

I0503995

+ Tutorial and winning strategies

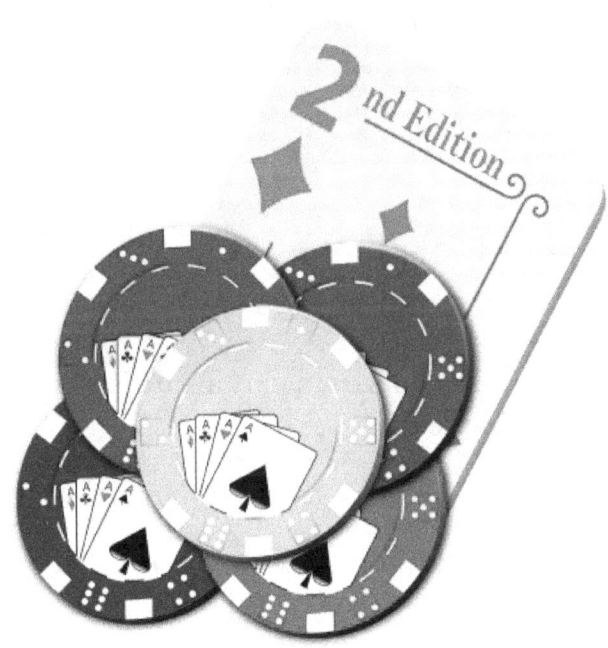

"Anyone who understands that poker really isn't a card game will have won the biggest prize."

Fabio Silva - CEO of Litoral Poker Brazil

www.litoralpoker.com.br

SUMMARY

PREFACE

INTRODUCTION

PREFACE

When I was still in the third year of my first degree in 1997, I had a teacher teaching Human Resources classes, I took with me some advice he gave to students, one of them was for us, after we took our diploma instead of Closing our eyes and plunging into the profession of Accountant or Auditor was to keep updating ourselves, even preparing us for new professions, for in his view, in twenty years or less, there would be new professions and ours would be extinct.

I pasted degree in 1999, but early on just opening a technology company with a friend, and 22 years of age , me to r nava a small business owner, not exercising the profession of accountant, although it has participated in some tenders for tax of the federal revenue. But the wind of technology hit me hard, and our technology company, after a few years, became a reference in the region.

In the middle of 2009, a friend introduced me to the online poker game, a big news and for me, from the first day, I noticed a business opportunity, because of a research and quickly realized that it was not a game of chance. In the first week, I looked for books about poker to buy, because I even had some content on the internet, but it wasn't much yet. I was fortunate enough to understand poker logistics quickly, so much so that the first books I bought dealt with poker psychology, which was one of the reasons I developed the emotional intelligence to practice the sport of mind that was already proliferating very quickly.

In 2011, I already had poker as an extra income and I started to project something bigger, not only as a player, but with an eye on the gaming industry, which at the time was among the three in the world, behind only the automobile and oil companies, I ended up founding a poker content production website , www.litoralpoker.com.br and then the Litoral Poker Brazil Youtube channel.

In mid-2015 I made a decision, professionalized myself in poker and left all other activities as extra income, so I devoted myself to playing professionally , seeking partnerships with major online poker platforms and boosting my YouTube channel . And it worked, even with some difficulties at the beginning, as in any change of direction in professional projects.

Some facts during the year 2016 added to my life new projects . My wife at the time was in law school and sometimes came back from university upset, when I asked what had happened, she told me that when she said she had a professional poker player husband, people scoffed, even teachers, that poker was a misdemeanor. criminal, unlawful act. I, at that time, had no intention of going back to law school because I had a semester in 2009, but I told her that when she finished she would go back to the course to show that poker was not illegal but a sport that could become a business.

It sounded like dreamer talk at the time, but I was always a fighter above all else, so I was already promised and it became a goal for me.

It was at my wife's Graduation Ceremony that the new project started in my life. For a magical reason, the Dean of the University present at the ceremony was my teacher twenty years ago, Professor Victorino, who said that in twenty years or less there would be professions that at that time did not exist. Moment that moved me a lot, because I had graduated in the city of Taubaté and the ceremony was in Caraguatatuba, being another city and another University, that is, a moment that meant a message to me, since I saw myself as a professional football player. poker, a profession that was not even foreseen in 1997 in Brazil , in front of the teacher who talked about it at the time.

A new project started in 2017, when I enrolled in law school and started studying poker and its academic application, as I was aware that the fundamentals of poker were already a discipline at UNICAMP in Brazil and Harvard and MIT in the United States for over fifteen years. Early on I designed my CBT on this theme, until in 2018 one more driving fact happened.

In 2018, attending the Judicial Mediator training course, taught by the instructors of the National Council of Justice (CNJ), I was invited by them to give a mini lecture on the application of Game Theory, which was a module of the course and was developed. by mathematician Jonh Nash based on the poker game.

It was another magical moment for my project, as I realized that it was not necessary to wait until the presentation of my TCC to develop another work with poker, the academic approach that always interested me.

Studying the subject, I soon realized that poker strategies or Game Theory were already inserted in the legal field, but for incomplete works, because there are few professional poker players who turn to the legal field , ie lack experience to exhibition of works on this theme.

In July 2019 I published my first book, "Poker, From Leisure to Business," focusing only on themes that were already in my domain, the game of poker itself and the target audience who were already playing poker.

In October 2019, I was invited by the Coordinator of the Law Course at Cruzeiro do Sul University, Pole de Caraguatatuba-SP, Dr. Marcelino Sato Matsuda to launch the book at the University in November 2019.

So I decided to anticipate a part of the content of what would be the my project, with an approach broader than poker game and its application in C i ences J Legal Entities , l publishing the "Poker, leisure to business - 2nd Edition" .

In this 2nd Edition, all the concepts necessary for the practice of poker were presented in a profitable way, and the profit in the poker game can be understood from various perspectives, closely connected with the purpose of each player. From those who play for fun, who play for the study of new business tools, to professional poker players.

INTRODUCTION

The term "professional gambler" is still not well understood, as many people believe that poker is lost more than what is won, but to clarify this question, just imagine which profession one works for, usually, none. No professional works to lose money. So when a player has poker as a profession, that means he has an income in the activity and may have periods of loss, as in any other profession or business activity. A more accounting answer would be that the professional gambler will always make a profit at the end of a financial year, which can be monthly, quarterly or yearly. Also, as already mentioned, it is possible to be a profitable player without having your main source of income in the game, in this case it is not because it is profitable that you will be called a professional player.

In " Poker, from leisure to business ," it will be the appropriate opportunity for those interested in learning about this "new" game that spans the five continents of the planet, in various social classes and which constantly draws attention, whether on sports TV channels, internet or live poker clubs.

They will be addressed all aspects of the game, such as legal, tax, academic and psychological, as well as presented a basic tutorial and winning strategies for orientadar people in the practice of this sport of the mind that more has grown in recent years.

CHAPTER 1

THE POKER GAME STORY

We will never know exactly where poker came from, but the biggest consensus for game scholars has come to the old Persian game called "As Nas", which must have been taught to Europeans by the excellent sailors who were Persian sailors.

Investigating "As Nas", it was perceived to be a game very similar to poker, where there is a hierarchy of games and familiar hands, such as pairs, broken and full houses.

The name "poker" may have come from other not-so-similar games such as "poque" (in French) or "pochen" (in German), which simply means "beating". Another game with a certain similarity, from the same time, that appeared in Europe, is the Spanish "first". This modality has also been researched further and actually has certain similarities in the hand hierarchy, but it is already a much more complicated and even a bit confusing game.

The earliest archives that refer to the most current poker seem to locate the game around the year 1830, by the region of New Orleans, an American city with great French influence. Early descriptions of poker in New Orleans show us that the game was almost always half deck, using only about 20 cards.

History seems to prove that the explosion of poker took place from this moment on, when it came to appear on steamers from the Mississippi River region, migrating with the gold rush pioneers to the American West. From there comes all that mythology around poker and cowboys, which is still used today in movies like "Meverick" and in country music.

Just as modern poker was born in the center of the United States and migrated to the west, the variants of the sport were slowly emerging and spreading throughout the country through large migrations. The second was the American Civil War, which through the soldiers came to the east and then took over the country.

At that time the full deck was introduced and the flush was created to later invent draw poker, card stud and straight.

Already closer to the turn to 1900, Americans created games with the joker, and spli high-low modalities. Community card games, Texas precursors and Omaha, were born only around 1925. It was then that, with World War II, American poker traveled again with the soldiers and embarked on the battlefields, especially in England, France. and with much greater might he seized Asia.

Since then, poker has been discreet in the American and world imaginary as a game of westerns, sailors and soldiers, and only took shape in the 1970s with the creation of the World Series of Poker (WSOP).

The invention of internet poker has truly exploded the sport as one of the biggest pastimes and competitive games on the planet.

Source: Brazilian Texas Hold'em Confederation
http://www.cbth.org.br/texas-holdem

CHAPTER 2

PRATICE POKER GAME BEFORE THE BRAZILIAN LAW

It is necessary to give a brief explanation of the development of pr will ethics of the game of poker in Brazil, because until recently, was considered a misdemeanor, for still frame as gambling.

In 2010, the International Federation of Sports of Mind (IMSA) officially recognized poker as a sport of the mind. With this, the entity confirmed poker as a game of skill, as well as chess, bridge, checkers and other sports that are part of IMSA. In Brazil, this recognition came two years later, in 2012, after several lawsuits in which expert reports were requested, as the report requested by the Delegate of the 27th Police District of São Paulo to the Criminalistics Institute of the Public Security Secretariat (SSP). P aulista, in which it addressed issues such as the game mechanics, terminology and technical issues. In it, the expert Adriano Yonamine concluded, for the second time, that poker is a game of skill, the first was in 2006, with advice from Professor Ricardo Molina's Laboratory of Expertise , which had also reached the same scientific answer. In short, gambling is one in which the luck factor influences 50% or more in the final result of the event, where the player cannot interfere with the final result by applying technique or skill. Since then, as has already happened internationally, the Ministry of Sports has also recognized the sport with the mind and put an end to the legitimacy of poker in Brazil.

Below is one of the reports mentioned above:

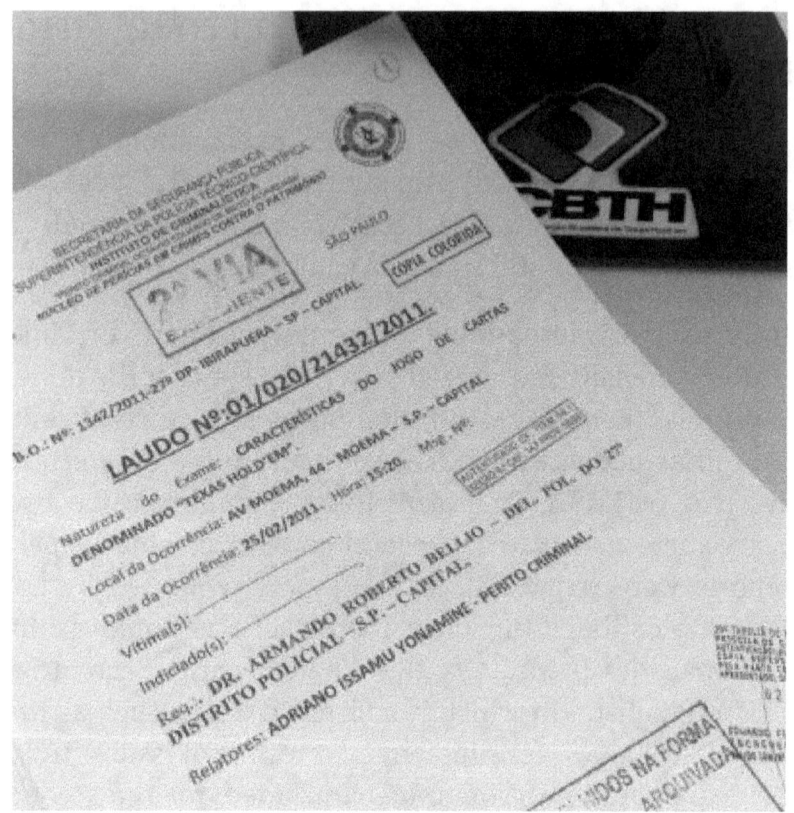

In analyzing Art. 50 of Decree Law No. 3688 of October 3, 1941, which deals with the exploitation and practice of gambling:

> "Art. 50. Establish or operate gambling in a public place or accessible to the public, with or without the payment of admission: (See Decree Law No. 4,866, dated 10.23.1942) (See Decree Law 9.215, dated 4.30.1946)

Paragraph 3. The following are considered to be games of chance:

a) the game in which the win and the loss depend exclusively or mainly on luck;

(b) horse racing bets outside the racetrack or where they are authorized;

c) bets on any other sporting competition.

Paragraph 4. For the purposes of criminal proceedings, the following shall be considered as a place accessible to the public:

(a) the private house in which gambling takes place, when persons who are not members of the family of the household usually participate in them;

b) the hotel or collective housing, whose guests and residents are provided with gambling;

c) bets on any other sporting competition.

c) the registered office or dependency of a company or association in which gambling takes place;

(d) the establishment intended for the operation of gambling, even if such a destination is disguised ".

Confronting the information that poker is a game of skill, that the end result is not predominantly luck, with § 3 (a) we have the exclusion of the game from criminal offense. Even so, over a period of time there has been a question from some legal operators regarding point "c" of the same paragraph 3, which includes "bets on any other sporting competition". It has been agreed that point "c" refers to bets on third party games, such as point "b", resolving the issue definitively in relation to the game of poker.

Perhaps the practice of poker in casinos in some countries like the United States, Uruguay, Argentina and others, has some induced form the lawmakers to label in the game of poker as a game of chance, since in casinos is practiced other games bad luck, such as roulette and bingo, which are games where the luck factor predominates.

Even after the decision that the practice of poker does not constitute a criminal offense in Brazil has been settled, sometimes the news of the closure of poker clubs is seen in the news, but the real reason for the ban is not known, often the practice or commercialization of other illicit acts. like bingo and slot machines.

The lack of regulation can also cast doubt on the legality of the game for those who are not well informed on the subject. However, it is interesting to note, for example, that the profession of journalist was no longer regulated in 2009 *, and was not unlawful because it was not regulated. In fact, there are professionals in the poker market who prefer the current situation, because the regulation could even hinder the practice of poker if done in a disorderly manner, for example, by regulating, it is established that competitions should be held exclusively in casinos.

Around the world, poker is regulated in some countries like Spain, Argentina, some states of the United States and unregulated in most, as in Brazil, but its practice is allowed even without regulation.

In the United States of America, online poker was banned in 2011 in the so-called "Black Friday" of world poker . Poker's "Black Friday" marked the blocking of operations from major sites such as Pokerstars, Full Tilt Poker and the Cereus network, which ran UltimaBet and Absolute Poker. The operation came from the US Department of Justice (DOJ), which accused websites of crimes such as money laundering, bank fraud and illegal operation in the United States.

After eight years, the poker market has rebounded, and in the United States, poker has been released in five states and the European market which had also suffered from the Spanish, French and Portuguese market closure (players were restricted to playing only within their respective countries), the so-called shared market began, where operating licenses are shared with more than one country, opening the possibility for a considerable increase in participants.

Returning to Brazil, the game of poker is becoming more and more popular in society, with hundreds of poker clubs spread across large cities and even in small centers, becoming a poorly enforced practice due to lack of regulation in law. On the contrary, it has been arousing the interest of a different part of society each year, due to the mystique of being a game that wins or loses a lot of money. It attracts business people, professionals like lawyers, doctors, judges, military and even jurists. In 2019, the number of poker players in Brazil is estimated at around 7.5 million competitors, according to data from CBTH (Brazilian Confederation of Texas Hold'em), the official entity of the category.

An interesting fact about online poker is that the credibility of an online poker platform is clearly linked to operating licenses in the United States, perhaps due to the strong oversight of government agencies that make the platforms safer for users, both financial liquidity (the amount of cash in the cashier should always cover player deposits), as in security of software and application fraud.

Currently the most well-known sites, Pokerstars, Full Tilt, 888 Poker, Partypoker, Black Chip Poker (WPN), Americas Card Room (WPN), Ya Poker (WPN) and Betfair Poker (Ipoker) operate legally in the USA.

More information about the mentioned rooms can be found at www.litoralpoker.com.br

*

https://noticias.uol.com.br/cotidiano/2009/06/17/ult57 72u4370.jhtm

STF decides that journalism diploma is not compulsory to practice

By 8 votes to 1, the Supreme Court (STF) ministers ruled in 2009 that a journalism degree would not be required to practice the profession.

The rapporteur Gilmar Mendes and the ministers Carmem Lucia, Ricardo Lewandowski, Eros Grau, Carlos Ayres Britto, Cezar Peluso, Ellen Gracie and Celso de Mello voted against the requirement of the diploma. Marco Aurélio defended the need for a higher degree in journalism for the exercise of the profession. Ministers Joaquim Barbosa and Carlos Alberto Menezes Direito were not present at the session.

For the rapporteur, damage to third parties is not inherent in the profession of journalist and could not be avoided with a diploma. Mendes added that untrue news is a serious misconduct and ethical problems that cannot be solved in the higher education of the professional. Mendes recalled that Decree-Law 972/69, which regulates the profession, was instituted under the military regime and had a clear purpose to keep journalists opposed to the regime from journalism.

Regarding the situation of the current higher education courses, the rapporteur stated that the non-compulsory degree does not automatically mean the closing of the courses. According to Mendes, journalism training is important for the technical preparation of professionals and should continue along the lines of courses such as cooking, fashion or sewing, where the diploma is not a basic requirement for practicing the profession.

Mendes also said that the media companies themselves should determine the hiring criteria . "Nothing prevents them from requesting a degree in journalism," he said. Read the full vote here.

Following the rapporteur's vote, Minister Ricardo Lewandowski emphasized the censorship character of the regulation. For him, the diploma was a "remnant of the regime of exception", which intended to control the information conveyed by the media, removing politicians and intellectuals opposed to the military regime from the newsrooms.

CHAPTER 3

POKER, FROM HOBBY TO BUSINESS

Image: Card Player Magazine Brazil

In 2010, the International Federation of Sports of Mind (IMSA) officially recognized poker as a sport of the mind. With this, the entity confirmed poker as a game of skill, as well as chess, bridge, checkers and other sports that are part of IMSA. In Brazil, this recognition came two years later, in 2012, after various models of the s court cases in which the expert reports were requested , mentioned in the previous chapter, that proved what was already known internationally, the Sports Ministries also acknowledged mode with the sport of the mind and put an end to the legitimacy of poker in Brazil.

As mentioned in the introduction, most poker players initially dream of becoming a professional gambler. The desire is so great that when disappointed with the game in normal moments, as a bad phase in both the game and the emotional, some end up giving up to practice as a hobby or sport, creating that rejection for something that could not be achieved. It would be like that attempt to conquer a person and failing it, comes out talking badly, as if it was her problem. The answer to this may be overstated expectation, but looking at this question coldly , it is easy to clarify.

Image: CardPlayer Magazine Brazil

The plurality of poker is perhaps the reason why it is rapidly proliferating in all regions of the planet, becoming an almost universal activity, even more because of the possibility of playing online. It is common to see final table tournament , almost all continents players, with different interests, for money, for fun or even for study.

Other people find in poker what they have never had in their lives, even people over 60 who have never won a trophy or medal in a sports competition . The pleasure of saying "I was a poker tournament champion with over a thousand people from around the world" has no financial value to pay. Even for those who only play poker by sport, it is possible to make a living out of the secret we will reveal in this book.

Poker as a business is like any business activity , requiring the investment of time, capital (bankroll) and study to get the return, the so-called ROI (return on investment). Even some concepts are the same between poker and traditional business , such as risk, expected value expectation (what long-term expected return) and the purpose of timeless activity. In both poker and traditional business, there is no end to the activity, a concept that justifies long-term results.

Q hen Christopher Bryan (Atlanta, November 21, 1975) became champion of the World Seri es of Poker in 2003, the game of poker began to be observed by the economic perspective, for a few reasons that drew attention at the time.

Cris was an amateur player until he became champion at the 2003 WSOP, when he became known as "Cris Moneymaker". Its title changed the course of poker after its victory, the sport of the mind has grown terribly, especially on the internet. The following year, the Main Event saw the number of entrants rise by 207%, and in 2007, 8,773 people entered the championship, a record that remains today.

Christopher completed his studies at Farragut High School and later graduated with a master's degree in accounting from the University of Tennessee. Before starting his poker career, he worked as an accountant in Tennessee.

Perhaps the biggest increase in poker popularity - specifically online poker - is due to a man's $ 40 online buy-in , leading to the history of the gaming industry. Chris Moneymaker qualified for the main event of the World Series of Poker through a small satellite buy-in event on the PokerStars online platform .

In the series, it survived a field of 839 participants - the largest in World Series of Poker history at the time. He faced some of the best known poker pros in the world - and won! Moneymaker's first place earned him $ 2.5 million, which wasn't bad considering it was his first live tournament.

After his victory, he quit his job and devoted himself exclusively to poker.

It's hard to believe that Cris Moneymaker's victory was a lucky wind that hit the amateur poker accountant, and today we know and can analyze the relationship between accounting and poker as a business.

Fabio Siva, "XDrPokerManX", the author of the book, is also a graduate of Accounting, perhaps the reason he started playing poker early in mid-2009 approached poker as a business. But initially, he preferred to keep poker as a favorite sport, even replacing Table Tennis, a sport that has devoted much of his life to that time as a player, president of a sports association and coach.

The following chapters will demonstrate the relationship between poker and the business world, from academia to the plicability of accounting science techniques for maximizing poker profits, as well as the ability to use strategies of the game in other professions.

C HAPTER 4

POKER'S GROUNDS IN UNIVERSITIES

Still in 2011, articles published in the United States, recruiters traders (stock exchange operators) said the poker market was very competitive, and that a good player who could win to survive in the game market for one term , probably it was good enough to operate in the financial market. At the time, a Los Angeles Times story reported that companies operating on Wall Street were recruiting poker players. Danon Robinson, one of the partners at Toro Trading, even claimed that a stock trader who was not interested in poker was a stranger to him. "It's like he doesn't read the Wall Street Journal."

In the book "The Professor, the Banker and the Suicide King" can observe the minutiae of the adventures of Texas banker Andy Beal, who was with the opponents , the biggest names in poker at the tables in Las Vegas on several occasions. Andy played such high values against them that he almost broke the pros, who pooled their bankrolls to duel with Andy Beal.

The poker player handles the pressure the whole time and the professional must always be attentive to s opportunities. In addition, it develops the ability to work with incomplete information, since they do not know the letters of s your s opponent s. You also have to change your decision with each new occurrence at the table, whether it is a hole card, a bet or a physical telegram (picture of the opponent's physical behavior). The stock trader also works with probabilities and should know when to invest or leave a business.

In the legal sciences, poker game strategies can be applied at the new institute that has gained in size in recent years, Mediation and Judicial Conciliation , as there is a time for negotiation and seeking to resolve the conflict with a lose and win between the parties, a good strategy can maximize the winning party's gain and minimize the losing party's losses.

The applicability of poker strategies to different professions may have contributed to universities placing a discipline that addressed the fundamentals of gambling in their curriculum. In the United States, at Harvard and MIT - Massachusetts Institute of Technology, the fundamentals of poker has been in place for over 15 years and in 2013, in Brazil, was introduced at Unicamp, the Faculty of Applied Sciences , Limeira campus and the University. from the São Francisco Valley (Univasf). Below is part of the first syllabus of the Fundamentals of Poker discipline at Unicamp in 2013:

In an interview with Época magazine, Charles Nesson, 69, Harvard Law Professor and founding president of the Global Poker Strategic Thinking Society (a group that brings together universities and aims to use poker to educate people), said the game, each increasingly popular around the world, it can develop skills such as patience, self-control and strategic thinking.

In addition, Poker is known to be the game of "bluffing" that nothing more is of a certain strength of representation of a game, as the law is often a representation must be made (simulation) of facts . It is common to hear of people in the legal area and the world poker: " You must tell ess the story right." This requires either developing or developing Emotional Intelligence, which can be transmitted by Universities through disciplines such as the Fundamentals of Poker.

4.1 Mathematical, psychological and academic aspects of the game - Game Theory

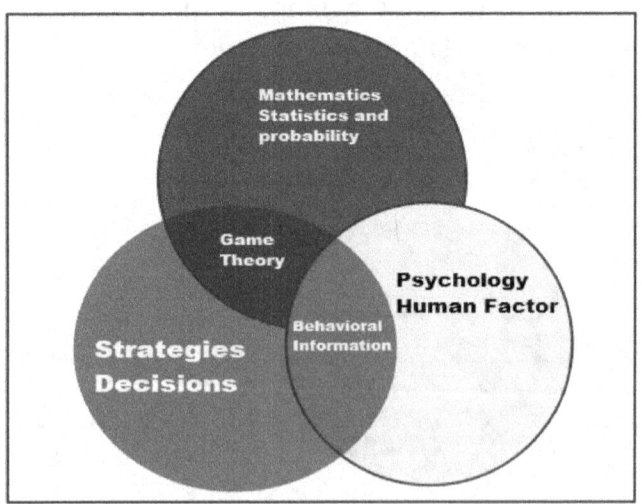

As already mentioned, the fundamentals of the game of poker is already a discipline at universities in the United States of America, undergraduate in law and in Brazil, at UNICAMP (State University of Campinas), since 2013, on the campus of Limeira / SP. In Brazil it is an elective course at the Faculty of Applied Sciences , often students of Engineering production and Manufacturing, Administration and the Public Administration, N utrição and Technology.

Also in Brazil, the Training Course of Judicial Indicators, the National Council of Justice (CNJ), also contains in its content programming, game theory, and was developed in part , by the mathematician John Nash , based on the game of poker .

Photo: John Nash / Card Player Magazine Brazil

Game Theory is already a relevant element in the legal field, with works such as the Guide to Criminal Procedure according to Game Theory, by the author Dr. Alexandre Morais da Rosa.

We can see that poker game strategies can be applied to both Exact and Social Sciences courses. This property , certainly if dev the human element that makes up the poker game, which roughly speaking , comprises about 30% of the structure, differing , for example , the game of chess, which is composed of 100% of mathematical factors . This feature of chess may perhaps be one of the reasons why it is far from academic, as it makes it a sport not very attractive to most children and adolescents. By the way, teenagers who like to play chess are called "nerds", generating a kind of bluster . Besides , it 's hard to meet a great chess player who became a millionaire, is n't it?

In poker, a player who is guided only by mathematics, can in medium and long term profitable results, but did not get a maximization of profitability, for it is necessary to apply strategies from psychological information from your opponents. Basically, players who play being guided only by mathematics , only take into account his own letters, without bothering with the actions and behavioral information from opponents, which most often convey important information , known as "tell s " or telegrams . Thus , mathematically, this player can not win or profit when he does not receive good cards, being exposed to a lucky factor, which in this case can reach 40%. In the long run, this player can make you a small profit, or even just a draw.

Some of you, even if they are not poker players, already must have seen some moves in televised games in which a player appears with a 70% chance of winning holding a pair of QQ (Checkers) , for example , and at the end of In this move, he loses to another player holding an AJ and hits an A on the last community card on the table, called the RIVER. This math is real, 30% chance for the opponent is a reasonable possibility, but 1000 repeated situations of this same play, the player holding QQ will win between 650 and 750 times, where he will have his profit in the long run.

Situations that the decision must be made based on mathematical concepts.

Although accurate mathematical concepts are not a condition for profitability in poker, there are situations that should be based on them for decision making. When behavioral information is lacking for analysis, this happens at a high frequency in multi-table tournaments when players are relocated, and it is common for one player to find himself dueling with another who has just sat at his table. In this case, if you do not have any other background information on the opponent's behavior, you should make decisions based on pure mathematics.

Is it possible to maximize profitability in poker without mastering math?

Yes! Math knowledge requirements are minimal, being more focused on the probability and statistics and also to read the numbers, that is, the interpretation is more important, because in the online game are applied tives (software) that perform the calculations for users, but the reading or interpretation is up to the player.

Bluffing is a strategy applied with psychological elements, as being a bluff, the chance of winning a hand when presenting your game is very small.

Example:

By playing a "22" pot against a player who has raised or raised you, with a board containing high cards such as Aces, Kings, even Q and J, you will most likely be playing against a winning hand mathematically, but depending of how to play, in position, raising, re-raising, ie playing in attack, bluffing! You can win the pot in your arm without reaching River and showing the cards of course! So it is important for you to know when you are playing for bluf or value

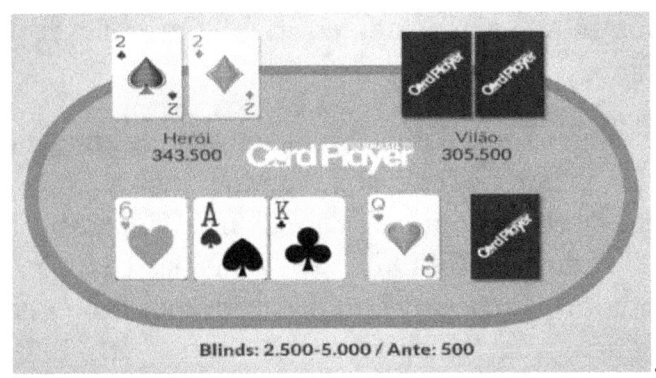

Heroí
343.500

Vilão
305.500

Blinds: 2.500-5.000 / Ante: 500

Photo: Annette Obrestad, cover of Card Player Brasil Magazine.

A fact which proved the importance of reading human behavior in the poker game was the victory Norwegian Annette Obrestad , and n 2007, surpassing 180 players without having access to his letters, as pasted a post it on the monitor, and played only with position and the betting pattern of the opponents.

We will have a chapter where we will discuss strategies to be applied for each player profile, and even in the online game it is possible to draw profiles, which are elaborated according to statistics of actions on the table, such as a player who participated 50 times. in 100 who had the opportunity, shows to be a player who plays with 50% of the possible cards of the deck, that is, likes to count on luck, since a strong game appears for each one, about 10% to 15% of the time. .

In short, poker is a game of people, behavior reading, role playing (simulation) and not cards. Therefore, having basic knowledge in mathematics contributes to the search for the best results , but it is not decisive in maximizing earnings.

Psychological aspects:

Now we will make a decision based on mathematical and psychological concepts in a situation of "ALL-IN" , the most famous poker move, when a player bets all his chips, winning can double or even triple his chips and losing , is eliminated from the tournament or losing all of your bankroll at the cash game table or similar mode.

This decision is more complex when the move is made before the FLOP, meaning the players involved in "ALL-IN" will watch the turn of the 5 community cards to know that m will win the chip pot.

Remember, no player has 100% to win the round, being the best possible situation when one holds a pair of aces, the famous "AA" (92%) and faces a player with "AK" (8%). However , there are several other settings, such as :

Hands - Probability of Victory (%)

A-Ko (59%)	X	7-6s (41%)
A-K (64%)	X	Q-J (36%)
2-2 (52%)	X	A-K (48%)
A-K (74%)	X	K-Q (22%)
A-A (92%)	X	A-K (8%)
A-A (82%)	X	K-K (18%)
A-A (82%)	X	2-2 (18%)
A-A (77%)	X	8-7s (23%)

But how can you use mathematical and psychological concepts to decision making that s situations ?

Let's say you're head to head with the world poker champion , he makes the ALL-IN move and shows you his pocket 99, you have an As and a T (10) in hand. This play defines his life in the tournament and his as well, as both have the same amount of chips, but it would not be the last chance for both of them, if there was a fold, FOLD, the amount of chips in both guaranteed would go a few more rounds.

You being an amateur player, with very little experience in the game, should not waste 44% chance to eliminate the world champion of poker , this time, even though less than 50% chance of winning. For we know that if the game continues iff , in a few hands you the chance to lose to it is huge!

Now, if you were the author of the motion d and All-in would be somewhat likely that the world champion would pay the bet , since 56% chance for it would not be a good neg idleness, p her experience, would know that in a few rounds eliminate you with less risk.

So we have the conclusion that mathematical and psychological information converge to better decision making, when not, it is very difficult for the gain to be maximized in the long run. Remembering that in the example above, players would no longer have to change the ending, just wait to beat all 5 cards on the table, see who would win the pot and collect the chips.

4 .2 Poker Strategies Applied to Legal Sciences

Although Game Theory initially developed as a tool in the field of Economic Sciences, today it is used in various academic fields, including the Legal Sciences.

In the Legal Sciences, Game Theory is applied directly to some institutes, such as Mediation and Conciliation, being an important tool in situations and negotiation between the parties to the dispute. The parties involved always seek what interests them, that is, they only care about their own gains, and the mediator should balance the result, so that no party is legally injured from the dispute or self-composition.

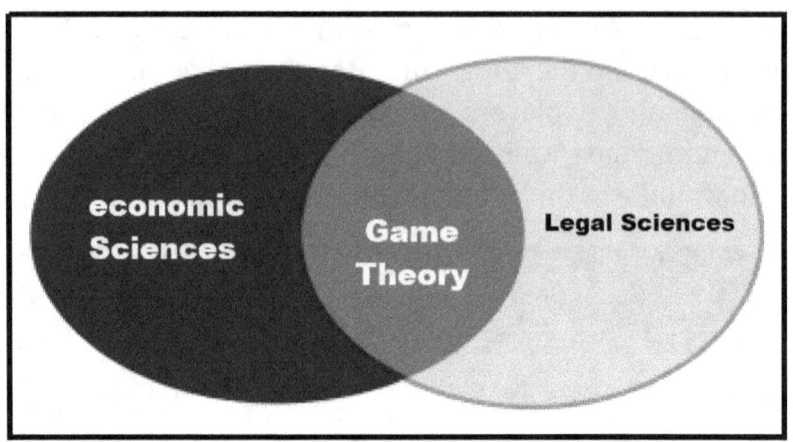

There are also situations in which decisions made in the economic realm generate consequences and outcomes in the legal realm, such as when companies choose to take the risk of paying court damages rather than preventing possible damages. We can take , for example , the huge amount of lawsuits involving telephone companies, in which they are most often condemned to indemnify consumers for moral and material damages.

Many have wondered why an international company prefers to pay compensation rather than improve or prevent such damages. The answer is quite simple based on the theory of games applied to the economic environment, companies seek the efficient balance between prevention and harm, generating the so-called efficient notion, in which they realize that they minimize their costs by paying eventual expenses in court damages, while rather than investing in prevention costs.

But now we have a question: What is the influence of the poker game in this context?

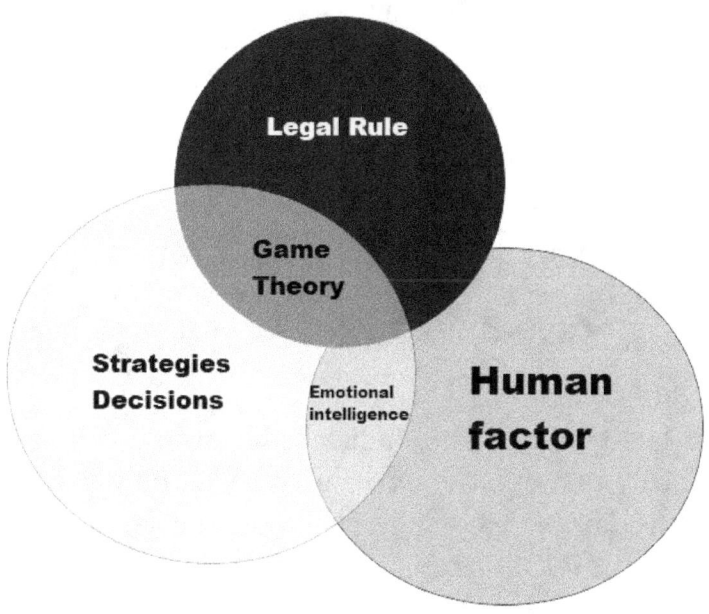

Initially, we have to label the legal sciences as a game, where norms are the rules, players are the parties who apply strategies in order to achieve victory, or literally, the positive outcome.

We have already seen that a poker player who relies solely on mathematical knowledge to make decisions can make a profit, but cannot maximize it efficiently, since disregarding emotional and human factors lacks information for decision making. more effective long-term results.

As a law graduate and Judicial Mediator, I can see the similarity between the poker player who only uses math and the lawyer who only relies on the legal norm to develop his legal pieces. In a logical analysis, this lawyer will only win when he holds the Law, and yet, not find a contradictory , in this case, an opponent with effective arguments. Penetrating even further into the psychological variable in the legal realm, the lawyer who scorns the behavioral information of the process is vulnerable to negative feelings that may act on himself, such as the ego that dominates him. A concrete example of this is when a lawyer advocates on his own, most often compromising his strategic decisions.

Relying solely on the norm can also undermine the outcome, such as losing the boundary of law, as the law of one party extends to the beginning of the law of the opposing party. In fact, this is when the litigation begins , because most of the time, the search for a right is driven by another negative feeling that undermines the result, revenge. It is normal for us to hear in a litigious divorce the phrase, "I want to take everything from him." In the poker game this feeling is also common, in a situation where players duel more than once in the same tournament and when they meet later, it generates what is called "META GAME", where the player without emotional intelligence compromises their decisions influenced by negative feelings like revenge.

But what would be the time to apply the strategies based on psychological information converging with the standard to maximize profit in the judicial process?

Recalling that in the game of poker, every time players reach the turn of the last community card in RIVER, luck can interfere with the end result. TURN being the last round for profit maximization and loss minimization without relying on luck.

I am very comfortable comparing the RIVER with the judgment given by the judge, which often ends up not satisfying either the winning party or not.

Thus, at the moment before the decision given by a third party, where the parties can still reach the maximization of the gain for those who have the right and the minimization of the loss for those who only defend themselves, it is essential to apply appropriate negotiation strategies based on on psychological information and legal norms. This is the reason that applies concepts of Game Theory in Judicial Mediation and Conciliation.

Fabio Silva, attending the Judicial Mediator Training Course, gave a lecture on aspects of Game Theory in poker right at a stage of the tournament, where players can make the "DEAL" deal. He explained how emotional factors and the analysis of mathematical and monetary information can contribute to negotiations aimed at maximizing gain and minimizing loss between the parties. He showed that in the win-lose game there can be a balance based on Game Theory, under the view of mathematician John Nash .

In **Chapter 11 - The "Deal",** the time of the agreement " , will be addressed in a practical way in poker, with the presentation of techniques emocioal intelligence necessary for success in this little discussed topic.

Photo caption: Fabio "XDrPokerManX", giving a talk on poker strategies applied to trading, at the Judicial Mediation Course of CNJ

- Brazilian National Council of Justice , December 2018, at the Ubatuba-SP Forum.

Now, away -If the subjective field of study and based on the practical application of the game of poker strategies in Judicial Mediation, for example, can apply one of the basic strategies of the game, which is always playing in position, or speak last in a negotiation. In the book, in the chapters dealing with poker strategies, details of this fundamental concept, "POSITION," will be exposed to achieve positive results. This strategy can be applied to both Judicial Mediation and economic business negotiations. Listening to the proposals, and then submitting a counter-proposal, is crucial to succeeding in finding the break-even point while remaining in the area of possible agreement. The part that first exposes its claim already draws a business boundary, often can be understood as an overestimated request .

Already in strategies based on Emotional Intelligence we can set an example, also in Judicial Mediation. Assuming a Mediation session where the parties are trying to share an inheritance in two equal parts, where it is possible through Emotional Intelligence, to identify that one of the parties has a selfish and clearly greedy behavior, being an individual who always wants to leave. Earning from a business. It could be proposed that the individual who demonstrated such behavior would make the two-part division as fair as possible for him, but the choice would be made by the other party as soon as the options are presented. That is, the selfish individual, even with the priority of his gain, would have to make the fairest division possible, because who would choose first would be the other party. Properly applying techniques derived from emotional intelligence can solve problems, making the parties feel satisfied with the negotiation, because one of the requirements for the success of a good Mediation is the satisfaction of both parties. good likelihood that the agreed will be met.

4.3 Artificial Intelligence X Emotional Intelligence

As I mentioned in the Foreword to this book, I had a teacher in the Accounting Graduate in 199 6 who told students not to settle in after receiving the diploma to work as Accountants or Auditors, as many professions would still be born and many would end in twenty years or less ...

Picture: pokerstars.com/blog/

Well, in 2019, I find myself professional poker player, a profession that did not exist, curs walk Law and interning in the area, as a law clerk . A normal situation if it were not the evolution of AI, which Anu n cia the end, in less than ten years, some professions, such as accountants, auditors and ... Legal Assistants

Artificial Intelligence, although developed in the field of games, its research and application extended to many other areas of the Humanities, as researchers initially used only games as a test base for the intelligence of a software or program, but eventually evolved to more sophisticated and complex types of logic.

I believe my teacher followed in 1997 the development of IBM's Deep Blue program designed to defeat then-world chess champion Garry Kasparov, which was already a harbinger of the evolution of Artificial Intelligence. Also because the machine won the first game against the world chess champion from the outset , but the match ended with a human victory in 4x2. Let's say it was already a considerable scare for humans, losing the first match of the much anticipated confrontation at the time.

Well, in the game of poker, machine life will not be so easy, perhaps because of the increased psychological factor that only humans are capable of mastering through Emotional Intelligence.

In 2007, in Vancouver, Canada, the "First Man-Machine Poker Championship" was held and won by humans. A year later, with a different set of human players, the machine won.

In 2017, other groups of researchers and developers at Carnegie Mellon University created software called Libratus, which playing heads-up matches beat four professional poker players in one match. In this case, the game of poker is not limited to heads-up play, most of the time it is played by multiple players, so this 1x1 machine win result should not frighten poker players so much.

The fact is that the advancement of Artificial Intelligence threatens the existence of various professions that have in their essence arithmetic and repeated activities, but provides professionals who master Emotional Intelligence with survival in the job market.

As already mentioned in this same chapter, the poker player deals with pressure all the time and the pro must always be on the lookout for opportunities. In addition, he develops the ability to work with incomplete information, since he does not know his opponent's cards, and has yet to change his decision with each new occurrence at the table, be it a tapped card, a bet or a physical telegram (image of the opponent's physical behavior).

In addition, Emotional Intelligence , which can be a tool for maximizing profitability in poker and other professions, unlike IQ, which does not change significantly over a lifetime, can evolve and increase. With some training and changing habits, it can be developed because it depends on the understanding of one's own feelings as well as the feelings of others. In short, it is possible for people to learn to read the behavior of others to make decisions and strategize for problem solving with incomplete information.

Therefore, it is very likely that the information contained above is the justification for the fundamentals of poker play being present in curricula at universities in the United States (Harvard and MIT - Massachusetts Institute of Technology) and Brazil since 2013 (UNICAMP and UNIVASF).

CHAPTER 5 - MAIN DIFFERENCES BETWEEN ONLINE POKER AND LIVE POKER

The answer to this question will depend on the goals you have in poker discussed in the previous chapter. If you play poker just for hobby, it is understood that money is neither a problem nor a desire for poker, so the live game ends up satisfying these players more because it has contact with other people, travels to various places not only to play, but also for sightseeing etc.

But it has been made clear by many professional poker players that online poker is the shortest path to profitability, as you don't have to spend on transportation, hotel stays, food and most of all with more time available for practice.

Example:

A player plays 10 stages of a live regional circuit during the year, spending an average of $ 2000 per stage between entry, transportation, food, lodging, and so on. It is known that reach the final table tournaments with over 100 entries is not for any player, and even taking into account that most of the prize is among the top three positions, the likelihood of this player, even coming to one final table during this same circuit, to be at a loss is very real.

In the online game, you can take on players from around the world within your own home or workstation, often being able to run parallel tasks within a space of time.

Most importantly, it is in online poker that we have the choice of poker platform deals and benefits that make it possible to reach our goal, reasonable profitability , or even lucrative fun.

Because with the proliferation of online poker already mentioned, poker rooms seek to retain their players in the quest to win preference.

However, it is important to note that the best option is dependent on the goals of each player, many play poker for fun or leisure, in this perspective, the live game can be more rewarding because it has a more effective social environment than online games.

So before you decide for yourself which mode would be most interesting, take a look at your goals, because if you choose to play online poker for extra income or exclusive winnings, nothing will stop you from playing live with friends for fun.

CHAPTER 6

I BEGINNING YOUR PATH IN POKER (TUTORIAL)

6.1 HAND RANKING

The ranking of the overall poker hands from highest to lowest follows. Note that in poker, suits have no values, values are numbers only, at times you might think that a ace of diamonds would be worth more than an ace of spades, but not ok. IMPORTANT, in Texas Hold'em, our choice, the games are made up of 5 cards, as each player is dealt 2 cards , the game is formed with 3 more community cards, and can use 4 community cards and up to 5, but in this case if the best game is 5 community cards, it will be for all players involved in the pot. So if the game reaches the last one, RIVER, it does not enter game 2 of 7 (2 of the player's hand and 5 of the table).

Royal Straight Flush - 10-JQKA all in the same suit.

Straight Flush - straight of five cards of the same suit, in order, such as 2-3-4-5-6 all diamonds.

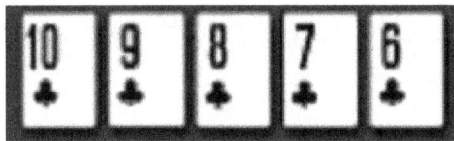

Four of a Kind - "court " - 4 equal cards, KAAAA, such as.

Full House - A set of three of a kind plus a pair, such as 8-8-QQQ.

Flush - five cards of the same suit

Straight - Five card straight , not necessarily of the same suit, as 6-7-8-9-10

Three of a Kind - "three of a kind" - three cards of the same rank, such as 10-10-10

Two pair - four cards with two of the same rank and the other two of the same rank, such as 8-8 and AA

One pair - two cards of the same rank, as 2-2

High Card - any card with the highest value

Designations for specific hands :

AA - American Airlines, Bullets, Pocket Rockets

AK - Big Slick, "Walking Back to Houston"

AJ - Ajax

KK - Cowboys

KQ - Wedding

KJ - Kojak K-9 - Canine QQ - Dames, Divas, Ladies, The H Sisters Ilton QJ - Independent, Oedipus Q-7 - Ha JJ Computer - Joker, Hooks

J-5 - Jackson Five, Motown

10-5 - Five and Ten Cents

10-2 - Doyle Brunson

8-8 - Snowmen, Octopuses

7-7 - Hockey Sticks, Walking Sticks

7-2 - The Hammer

5-5 - Nickel, done

5-4 - Jesse James (by his Colt .45)

4-4 - Sailboats

2-2 - Ducks

6.2 Vocabulary of Poker

Ace-High A five card hand that has no hand combinations (flush, straight, pair, etc.), but contains an Ace.

All-in When you bet all of your money on one hand, either voluntarily on the belief that you have the strongest hand, or because you don't have enough money to cover the full amount bet by someone else. You then play the pot for an amount proportional to what you contributed.

Ante The minimum bet that players must place in the pot for each player before starting to bet. The ante is placed before any cards are dealt.

Bad Beat When a good hand that would be expected to win the pot is won by a draw.

Backdoor making a hand you weren't playing, for example. You play for a full house, but you flush

Big Blind The first bet placed by the player to the left of the player who throws the small blind. It is a forced bet. The value of the big blind bet is equal to the lowest bet. For example, in a $ 10 to $ 20 game, the big blind is $ 10.

Big Slick An AK combination as pocket cards.

Blind Bet A forced bet that is placed before any card is dealt. It is considered a live bet for the first round of betting. You have big blind and small blind bets in the first betting round.

Bluff Pretend you have a better hand than you really do, betting aggressively in the hope that the other players will fold.

Bullets A pair of aces. If these are your pocket cards, they are also known as "Pocket Rockets".

Burning a card - Discarding the card from the top of the deck.

Buy-in Amount of the amount you must bring to a game.

Call When you place a bet equal to the previous bet.

Withdraw To finish playing and exchange your chips for cash.

Check -   When you want to stay in the game but do not place a bet. You can only verify that no other bets have been placed in the betting round.

Check-Raise To check at the beginning of a betting round and then raise when a player to your left bets.

Community Cards - Cards that are dealt to the table. All players can use these cards to complete a five card hand.

Dead Man's Hand Two pairs have d consisting of Aces & Eights. This is said to be the hand that Wild Bill Hickock was holding when he was shot dead.

Dealer Button A flat disc that is used to indicate the dealer position at the table in online poker. The disk is usually marked with a D.

Deuces A pair of two (22) .

Family pot When everyone at the table is still involved in the pot

Flop The first three community cards dealt on the board

Fold When players play their cards. They give up any complaints about the pot in exchange for not having to contribute more money to the pot.

Forced Bet A bet that a player has no choice but to make, a blind bet

Gut Shot , in Brazil the famous "drill" - when a letter is missing in the middle of a straight.

Flush Draw When a player holds four cards of the same suit and expects to draw a fifth card of that suit to complete a flush.

Heads-Up - better known as HU - a contest with only two players.

Hole Cards These are the hole cards in front of the players. (Also known as "Pocket Cards")

Kicker   - The highest unpaired card in a player's hole cards. Example:

One player has AK in hand and the other has AQ, at the table turned A 5 8 9 4, both have pocket A, but kicker K is greater than Q.

Monster - A very strong hand.

Muck - When you don't want to show your hand to the table. The hand is discarded without being displayed on the table. You can play a losing hand in a show down or the winning hand if everyone else folds before you.

Nuts - The best possible hand that cannot be won at a specific point in the game.

Nut Flush - A flush containing the Ace.

Outs - Cards that can flip at the community table to complete a game. Example: A player has a pair of 55, as he has 4 cards 5 in play, he has 2 outs to form a set.

False Pair - A pair at the table larger than your pocket pair. Example: A player has 22 hands on the table has 4 4 8 k 8 Q, in which case the table already has 2 pairs, 4 and 8, which are larger than the pair of 22 in the player's hand. If the other opponents do not have any higher pair or no A, this play will draw as there is the 5-card game: 2 pair, 4 & 8, and kicker K.

Brothers - Letters with pictures, examples: K - king, Q - ladies and J - jacks. Picture cards (King, Queen, Jack).

Hand cards - The hole cards dealt face down to each player, in this case 2 cards. (Also known as "Hole Cards")

Pocket Rockets - A pair of aces as your pocket cards. (hole cards).

Pot - is the stack of chips that accumulates as each player bets, bets and raises. All winnings are paid into the pot. The value of the pot varies. It depends on the bets involved and the amount wagered by the players. The pot goes to the winner of each round.

Note: The house receives a small percentage of the pot. This is known as rake or commission. In tournaments, the house receives a commission from the tournament entry value called BUY-IN (entry) + fee, for example a tournament of $ 50 + $ 10, $ 50 goes to the prize pool with the payment of all players and $ 10.00 is the commission of the company that organizes the tournament.

Pot Limit - It is a game mode that the value of each bet will only be up to the maximum value of the current pot per round. A game where a player's maximum bet is pot size.

Rainbow - When the board contains 3 or 4 cards of different suits.

Ring Game - A normal real money table game, unlike a tournament game. In the tournament, an entry fee is paid as a sign up and chips are received, which varies according to the rules (structure) of each tournament.

River - This is the last of the community cards to turn, if no other player folds to the river, opponents show their cards and whoever has the best game wins the pot.

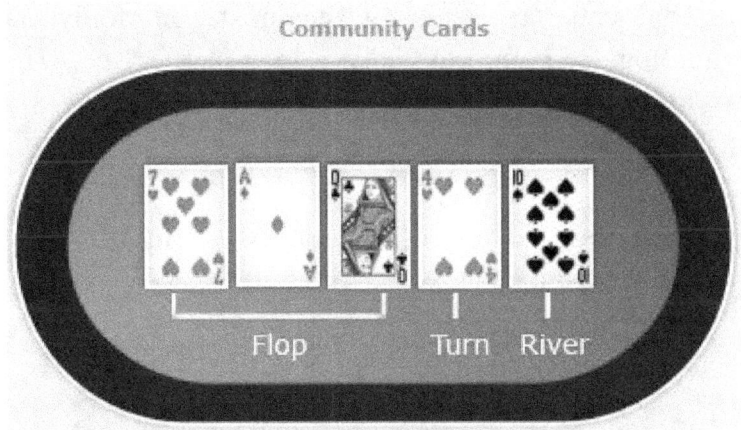

Semi-bluff - To bluff with a hand that still has the potential for luck and can improve to be the winning hand.

Seven Deuce - The weakest starting card combination in Texas Hold-em (7-2)

Small Blind - The first bet placed by the player to the left of the dealer. It is a forced bet. The amount of the small blind bet is equal to half of the highest bet . For example, in a $ 10 to $ 20 game, the small blind is $ 10.

Tigth Player - A tight player is a player who never goes into a pot unless he has a good hand.

Under the Gun - Known as "UTG" - The player who must act first in the betting round.

Now that you have some of the most commonly used terminology at hand, let's take a look at the Texas Hold 'Em game.

6.3 Expected Values in Poker (EV) - Definition and Strategies

Expected Value

Explanation

Expected value (or EV) is the metric used to describe the profitability of the poker decision. An expected value can be positive, neutral or negative. A negative expected value implies a loss.

The expected value of simple poker scenarios can be calculated using a simple formula.

Let's look at using the formula illustrated with an example of Hold'em.

We are on the turn facing a $ 50 all-in bet in a $ 100 pot. We expect to have about 40% of the pot over our opponent's range. What is the expected value of a call?

Let's start by defining the four variables that make up the formula for the expected value.

Likelihood of winning - 40%

Likelihood of Losing - 60% Value of

win - $ 150 (Which is in the middle, plus the villain bet).

Amount lost - $ 50 (our investment)

Let's connect the variables in the EV formula. Note that percentages must be expressed in "decimal" format (divide them by 100 first).

$$(0.4 * \$ 150) - (0.6 * \$ 50) = EV$$

When dealing with brackets, it is important to always calculate the value of brackets before performing any other mathematical function.

$$(\$ 60) - (\$ 30) = \$ 30$$

So we should expect to earn $ 30 on average every time we make this call. This is because, according to our pot odds, we should have a profitable call as long as we have more than 25% equity.

Advanced EV Calculations

The above calculation is a very simple EV calculation example. It was relatively simple for at least two reasons:

1) We do not take into account variables further, as fold-equity

2) Our choice is "all-in", which means that we should not take into account variables complex on the river.

Let's look at a slightly more complex example, where we need to consider the pot value and the fold value.

There is $ 100 in the middle on the turn. We semi-bluffed all-in for $ 50. We expected to have 20% equity when we called and expect our opponent to give up about 30% of our bet time. What is our expected value?

One way to solve these types of problems is to break them down into all their possible outcomes, along with their respective profit / loss.

Event A - Villain folds and we won the $ 100 pot. (Happens 30% of the time).

Event B - The villain pays and we win $ 150. (It happens (0.7 * 0.2) 14% of the time).

Note that we can establish the probability of successive events (ie, called villains and then win) by simply multiplying their respective probabilities together (when expressed in decimal format). Our opponent pays 70% of the time against our bet and we will suck on the river 20% of the time. Consequently:

$0.7 * 0.4 = 0.14 = 14\%$

Event C - The villain pays and we lose our $ 50. (It happens ($0.7 * 0.8$) 56% of the time).

EV's basic formula can be expanded to include separate support for each event.

EV Formula - Let's enter the information about the three events in a three square formula.

$(0.3 * \$ 100) + (0.14 * \$ 150) + (0.56 * \$ -50) = EV$

Note that the bracket representing the C-event uses a negative integer to show losses.

$(\$ 30) + (\$ 21) - (\$ 28) = \$ 23$

The semi-bluff turn, therefore, still generates a positive expected value of $ 23, despite the fact that we have less equity than in the first example. This helps illustrate the value of folding equity when we play our draws aggressively rather than passively. If we were facing a turn bet in the above example, instead of betting ourselves, we would not be getting the right price for a + EV (positive expected value) call.

Range building software

he above level of complexity is presumably the limit for humans to calculate manually. It's not that humans don't have the ability to handle more complex scenarios, it's simply a matter of practicality. It makes no sense to perform long calculations by hand when we have the option of generating accurate expected values for complex game trees with the benefit of computer assistance.

The most popular commercially available software designed to calculate the expected value for complex game trees is CardrunnersEV. (Note that a game tree is simply a diagram detailing all possible actions that can be taken during a poker hand - they can get very big very quickly).

Strategy Application

A solid understanding of the expected value is important for a high level game. Good players not only know which moves are likely to have a positive expected value, but can also give you a rough idea of exactly how profitable those moves are. Beginning players may be able to guess the best line, but they are usually pressured to make an accurate EV estimate.

Let's look at a very simple example of this (one in which the precise LV must be known without calculation).

The villain goes all-in for $ 50 into a $ 100 pot on the turn. We expect to have 25% equity and make the call. Calculate the following -

a) The expected value of a call.

b) The expected value of a fold.

c) Estimate the expectation for the general hand.

a) We are getting the precise pot odds we need because we have 25% pot of capital. This means that our expectation will be precisely 0.

b) Folding always has an expectation of 0. It is extremely important to understand that this expectation of 0 is relative to the current decision point. This does not mean that we are tied with the whole hand.

c) Many players have mistakenly assumed that our expectation is 0, since we made a draw call with our draw. Although this describes our relative expectation , it does not describe our expectation for the overall hand (absolute expectation).

The expectation for our overall hand will depend on how much we have invested in the pot so far. Since there is already $ 100 in the middle and we are in a heads-up pot, it is reasonable to estimate that we have already invested approximately $ 50 in the pot. Our expectation for the overall hand is therefore - $ 50 (negative $ 50).

Relative versus absolute expectation

It is important to differentiate between relative and absolute expectation when discussing expected value. Many players may be surprised to learn that making a draw call results in a loss to the overall hand. This does not mean that calling is a mistake, simply that the cards fell favorably on our opponent and we ended up losing. Although we have some measure of control over our relative expectation, our absolute expectation is usually just a measure of how well we are doing during a given hand.

Max-EV vs + EV

Being able to make rough estimates of our EV is useful because it allows us to make distinctions between two profit lines. It is possible in poker for more than one option to generate a positive expectation. In such cases, a good player always selects the line that has the highest expected value - described in the industry as "max-EV".

https://www.888poker.com/magazine/poker-terms/expected-value

6.4 The basic math of poker, the probability

Understanding math is essential. When there is numerical understanding, it is easier to deal with bad beats and bad phases.

First, let's take a look at the chances of receiving certain hands:

Mãos	Probabilidade de receber (%)
A-A	0,45
J-J, Q-Q ou K-K	1,3
6-6, 7-7, 8-8, 9-9 ou 10-10	2,2
2-2, 3-3, 4-4, 5-5	1,8
A-K do mesmo naipe	0,3
A-K de naipes diferentes	0,9
A-Q ou A-J do mesmo naipe	0,6
A-Q ou A-J de naipes diferentes	1,8
A-X do mesmo naipe, sendo X qualquer carta menor que J	2,7
A-X de naipes diferentes, sendo X qualquer carta menor que J	8,1
Qualquer par	5,8
Quaisquer duas cartas do mesmo naipe	23,5
Quaisquer suited connector	2,1

Now, let's look at winning odds when there is a preflop all-in, with the table below, we can see that an AK losing to a 7-6s is no big deal. On the other hand, we may realize that the best pre-flop all-in situation is when our AA encounters an opponent's AX.

Mãos	Probabilidade de Vitória (%)
A-Ko x 7-6s	59 x 41
A-K x Q-J	64 x 36
2-2 x A-K	52 x 48
A-K x K-Q	74 x 22
A-A x A-K	92 x 8
A-A x K-K	82 x 18
A-A x 2-2	82 x 18
A-A x 8-7s	77,5 x 22,5
A-T x K-Q	59 x 41
A-2 x J-T	54 x 46
A-Q x K-J	62,5 x 37,5
J-J x A-5s	66,7 x 33,3
A-J x 9-4o	68 x 32
A-J x 6-4s	61 x 39

With the help of the table below , you can see that with two cards of the same suit, we will hit a flush on the flop less than once every one hundred hands, and a flush draw about eleven times every one hundred hands. Going a step further, assuming that a flush draw on the flop is completed, up to the river a little more than once every three hands, it follows that the flush will be completed, up to the river, three times in a hundred hands played.

Jogo	Porcentagem (%)
Um par	26,7
Dois pares	2,0
Um par ou melhor	32,43
Trinca	1,35
Trinca com um par na mão	11,76
Sequência	1,31
Draw para Sequência	9,6
Flush	0,84
Flush Draw	10,85
Flush House (um par na mão)	0,70
Full House (com duas cartas não pareadas)	0,10
Four (com um par na mão)	0,24
Four (com duas cartas não pareadas)	0,025
Straight Flush (8-9s ou 7-9s)	0,02
Straight Flush (9-6s ou 9-5s)	0,01
Royal Straight Flush	0,000015

So if you have the habit of calling with suited cards, to try to hit the flush, you need to rethink your strategy. Pre-flop money does not make up for the low probability that we will postflop the flush.

Stop and review these tables numerous times. It was from the most basic mathematics that most major strategies emerged.

6. 5 Pot Odds and Outs

What are the differences between poker odds and poker outs and how do they affect your game? Here are the answers to all your questions about poker outs and poker odds.

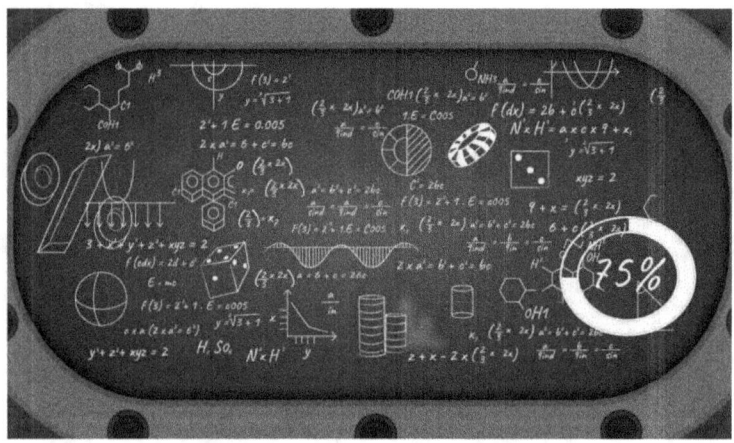

To play virtually any casino game and succeed, some knowledge of math is required. But no casino game requires more knowledge and application of math than poker. The two most significant mathematical indicators of poker success are odds and outs. This article will explore both in some detail to give the reader a good insight into what they are and why they are important.

ODDS

Simply put, odds are the odds, for or against, of the player making a certain hand. If a player has four cards of a flush (color), the odds or odds of completing the flush are estimated at approximately 4 to 1. The numbers can be a bit confusing. This does not mean that the player has 1 in 4 (25%) chance of completing the hand. It means that of five hands, one hand will complete the flush and four will not complete. So 4 to 1 odds means that the player will complete 1 flush in about 5 hands or about 20% of the time. Remember that mathematical poker odds are calculated over the long term. In the short term, a player may complete a flush when he has four of a suit for four, five or more hands in a row, or passes 15, 20 or more poker hands without ever completing a flush.

Poker hand with a flush draw (incomplete flush) and another hand with a straight draw incomplete sequence) with flops showing both draws.

Some players find it easier to use percentages, while others prefer to use odds. Let's look at some examples of converting odds to percentages.

2 to 1 against is the same as one in three, so 100/3 = 33.3%.

3 to 1 against is the same as one in four, so 100/4 = 25%.

4 to 1 against is the same as one in five, so 100/5 = 20%.

5 to 1 against is the same as one in six, so 100/6 = 16.7%.

How about the opposite, ie the odds percentage?

33% - 100/33 = 3, so 3 - 1 = 2 making 2 to 1 odds.

25% - 100/25 = 4, so 4 - 1 = 3 making 3 to 1 odds.

20% - 100/20 = 5, so 5 - 1 = 4 making 4 to 1 odds.

7% - 100 / 16.7 = 6, so 6 - 1 = 5 making 5 to 1 odds.

An alternative method of converting a percentage to odds is to divide the percentage of failing by the percentage of succeeding.

33%: 33% chance of getting it, 67% chance of not getting it: 67/33 = 2, making 2 to 1 odds.

25%: 25% chance of getting it, 75% chance of not getting it: 75/25 = 3, making 3 to 1 odds.

20%: 20% chance of getting it, 80% chance of not getting it: 80/20 = 4, making 4 to 1 odds.

7%: 16.7% chance of getting it, 83.3% chance of not getting it: 83.3 / 16.7 = 5, making 5 to 1 odds.

OUTS

To calculate odds, a poker player needs to know the number of outs. An out is just a short way of saying the number of cards left in the deck that will help you complete a hand. In the above example, of a four card hand of the same suit, the number of cards (or outs) that will complete a flush hand (colors) is nine, since each suit has 13 cards, four of those 13 cards are in the hand, leaving nine of the same suit.

Some common outs to play after the flop (where you have two down or "hole" cards and three common cards displayed) are shown in the table below. As they are very common, it is good to keep in memory.

Outs	Você tem	Você espera formar
2	Um par	Trinca
4	Dois pares	Full House
4	Inside Straight	Straight
8	Open Straight	Straight
9	Quatro de um Flush	Flush
15	Straight e Flush	Straight/Flush mais

The following table shows specific examples to help clarify how outs are determined.

As you can see from the tables above, counting outs is not too complicated. Even so, there are some things that should always be remembered.

Tipo de draw	Mão	Flop	Cartas Out	Nº de Outs
Par até Trinca (Set)	5♠ 3♣	K♦ 2♥ 8♣	3♥ 3♦	2
Uma overcard (maior que o flop)	A♥ 6♠	9♣ 3♦ 2♣	A♠ A♣ A♦	3
Inside Straight	8♥ 6♣	9♣ 5♦ Q♣	7♣ 7♣ 7♥ 7♦	4
Dois pares a Full House	Q♠ J♥	Q♥ J♠ 4♣	Q♣ Q♦ J♣ J♣	4
Um par a dois pares ou set	K♣ J♦	K♦ 9♣ 3♠	K♠ K♥ J♠ J♣ J♥	5
Nenhum par a um par	8♦ 6♣	2♣ 3♥ J♦	8♣ 8♣ 8♥ 6♠ 6♥ 6♦	6
Duas overcards a overpair	A♠ Q♣	9♥ 7♦ 3♣	A♣ A♥ A♦ Q♠ Q♥ Q♦	6
Set a Full House/Quadra	5♣ 5♦	5♦ 7♥ Q♣	5♥ 7♣ 7♣ 7♦ Q♣ Q♥ Q♦	7
Open Straight Draw	7♦ 6♣	5♦ 8♥ 2♣	9♣ 9♣ 9♥ 9♦ 4♣ 4♣ 4♥ 4♦	8
Flush Draw	Q♦ 10♦	K♦ 5♦ 7♦	2♦ a 4♦, 6♦ a 9♦, J♦ A♦	9
Inside Straight e duas Overcards	K♠ Q♥	J♦ 9♣ 3♣	J-todos, K♠ K♥ K♦ Q♠ Q♣ Q♦	10
Inside Straight Draw e Flush	A♠ K♣	J♣ Q♦ 2♣	10-todos, 3♣ a 9♣, Q♣	12

Outs cannot be counted twice. In the last row of the table above, there are 15 outs. There are only 15 cards that can complete a flush (straight) or straight (straight). If you do a quick head count, you can get 17 outs, 8 outs for a straight and 9 outs for a flush. Since the hand has a straight and flush possibility, an out may consider a straight and a flush in the count. In the example, A ♦ and 9 ♦ play a double role in completing a flush or straight. Beware of this when playing a live game. You don't want to assume that you are more likely to make a hand than you actually have.

Some outs will not help you win. Sometimes there are outs that improve the hand but don't help you beat it. Consider this hand as an example. You have 6 ♥ 5 ♠ and the flop is 7 ♣ 4 ♦ J ♣ . You want to form a straight and any 3 or 8 will come. But the flop also contains two clubs; so if you get 3 ♣ or 8 ♣ , you have a Straight, but someone might beat him with a Flush. In fact, you only have six good outs out of the usual eight outs. Do not assume that all outs are good and will help you. I always prefer to over-caution and just count the good outs. It makes no sense to put your hard-earned money at risk without knowing if you have the best possible chances of winning.

DETERMINING YOUR CHANCES IN POKER

Poker Odds and Outs

After calculating your good outs, you can determine your odds (odds or chances). The three ways to do this are shown below. The first method does not require calculations. See the table below. It shows the odds (chances) of forming your hand (based on your outs) from flop to turn, turn to river and flop to river.

Outs	Porcentage m	Odds	Porcentage m	Odds	Porcentage m	Odds
20	42.6	1.35-1	43.5	1.30-1	67.5	0.48-1
19	40.4	1.47-1	41.3	1.42-1	65.0	0.54-1
18	38.3	1.61-1	39.1	1.56-1	62.4	0.60-1
17	36.2	1.77-1	37.0	1.71-1	59.8	0.67-1
16	34.0	1.94-1	34.8	1.88-1	57.0	0.75-1
15	31.9	2.13-1	32.6	2.07-1	54.1	0.85-1
14	29.8	2.36-1	30.4	2.29-1	51.2	0.95-1
13	27.7	2.62-1	28.3	2.54-1	48.1	1.08-1
12	25.5	2.92-1	26.1	2.83-1	45.0	1.22-1
11	23.4	3.27-1	23.9	3.18-1	41.7	1.40-1
10	21.3	3.70-1	21.7	3.60-1	38.4	1.60-1
9	19.1	4.22-1	19.6	4.11-1	35.0	1.86-1
8	17.0	4.88-1	17.4	4.75-1	31.5	2.17-1
7	14.9	5.71-1	15.2	5.57-1	27.8	2.60-1
6	12.8	6.83-1	13.0	6.67-1	24.1	3.15-1

Using the table above, it is easy to see that if you have a flush draw after the flop (meaning you have nine outs), you have a 19.1% chance, or 4.22 to 1 against odds, of making the hand on the turn. With the turn and river still to come, you have a 35% chance (or 1.86 to 1 odds against) of getting the flush.

The next method for determining your poker odds is simply to do the math; It's easy to say, doing is a little more complicated. In fact, the calculations are so complex that it would be a waste of time and space to put them in this article. It would be a lot of work for me and you would probably fall asleep trying to keep up with the process; So let's move on.

Fortunately, there is a shortcut. Although not entirely accurate, it is enough to play poker. It's called the four and two method.

Multiply your outs by four if the turn and river are yet to come.

Multiply your outs by two if only the river is yet to come.

Using the same example as the flush draw, if someone goes all-in and you are guaranteed to see the turn and river cards, multiply your outs (nine) by four and get 36%. This calculation is slightly different from the graph, but very close, close enough to the game.

If there is only one card left, multiply your outs by nine and you get 18%. Again, not accurate, but close enough to the game.

www.litoralpoker.com.br

SUMMARY

That is all. Everything you need to know about poker odds and outs to form the foundation of a successful poker game. Obviously, it takes several other skills to become a successful poker player. They will be covered in future articles. For now, if you can understand and determine the right count of outs and remember the simple Method Four and Two to determine the win percentage, you're on the right track to have fun and profit from playing poker.

https://en.888poker.com/magazine/estrategia/poker-outs-e-odds-your-important-answer- questions

6.6 Concept by : Independent Chip Model , better known as " ICM "

ICM, also known as Independent Chip Model, is a mathematical formula used by poker players to calculate equity chips in a tournament. They use these calculations to make the best decisions in later hands or to decide how fair a deal is to split the tournament prize pool. Tournament chips have a relative value, meaning a big blind is worth more to the short stack than to the chip leader.

ICM is the calculation that will tell you how much your real money tournament chips are worth.

GIVE ME AN EXAMPLE

Imagine a $ 10 sit-and-go with nine players, which gives you a $ 90 prize pool. First place gets $ 45. Second place $ 30. Third place $ 15.

Each starts with 1,500 chips, which puts 13,500 chips into play. After an hour, there are only four players left. The blinds are at 100-200 and their stacks are:

John - 6,200

Mary - 3,900

Rafael - 2,600

Paula - 800

After calculating the ICM for each of the stacks, we can learn a lot about the best strategy for this bubble. For example, to protect his leadership, John will hardly call an all-in from Maria without an excellent hand. Rafael, on the other hand, would be making a big mistake calling an all-in with a marginal hand, since Paula has only four big blinds.

If the four players agree to make a deal, by ICM, the division would look like this:

John - R $ 33.06

Mary - R $ 27.24

Rafael - R $ 21.90

Paula - $ 7.80

As you can see, John's great leadership means his stack is worth a little more than the original second place prize. And despite being very short, Paula's chips still have significant value.

The calculation is different when calculated by chip chop, where its chip percentage is directly equivalent to the prize pool percentage. That is, John, who has 46% of the chips in play, would be entitled to $ 41.40. Already Paula, with only 6% of the chips, would have $ 5.40.

This shows why many players prefer ICM over chip chop deals (unless you're the chip leader). Of course they adjust the values according to the skill difference between the remaining competitors. ♠

6.7 ICM X EV - Definitions and Applications

Although they are different concepts, many players get confused when applying them.

In short, the ICM concept should be used in the final tournament phase just before the final table and is critical for decision making when there are very short players with few chips on the table. As a rule, the players with the most chips cannot be eliminated before those players by the concept of ICM. When we see a Chip Leader falling in 2 or 3 plays at a final table with shorts players, we say "this one murdered the ICM".

But is it possible?

Yes, suppose the Chip Leader gets involved in a second chip hand and loses most of his stack, and then loses the rest to other players. I have witnessed it myself.

Deciding to fold, folding, with a pair of aces, "AA", preflop only makes sense based on the concept of ICM, in two situations, one of which is in satellite tournaments. Ex: In a satellite tournament, with a player missing to win the entry (prize), you with the guaranteed almost 15bb seat, you get a pair of "bucks", the AA, and the player your right, with more chips, opens the pot with all-in. By the concept of ICM, it 's insta fold!

The concept of "EV" has no tournament phase to use, if the play has a positive EV, it may be applied, but may not be due to some information the player has about the villain, for example. There is , however , one observation, EV refers to long-term chip winnings (expected value) , and we know that chip winnings in the early stages of tournaments are not significant. So we always hear that one should play more aggressively in the middle and late stages in order to exploit the more passive opponents, where the effective chip gain is much higher by increasing the value of the blinds.

Are there situations that should only use EV concept?

Yes. In tournaments that win only first place, champion, the EV-oriented player of the play should be solely. The practical situation of this concept is in the games of SPIN AND GO, where only the award participates, the champion. So there is no point in folding, folding because you are out of second place and the third has only one blind.

So in this mode, if the play has positive EV, you must play 100% of the time!

6. 8 Red line, parameter for rating your game

As already mentioned, poker is not a game of luck, it is defined in continuous events by skill, that is, in a single event, the luck factor can make a difference in the outcome, but in an event set, this factor loses its way. predominance for skill. In other words, if a player who has more ability faces a player who plays randomly 100 times, the most skilled player is likely to win 60 times or more.

However, there is only one way to circumvent the luck factor more often, it is by winning pots of chips by making opponents fold before the river, without showing the cards, before comparing who has the best game to keep the chip pot. It seems obvious, but many people are still mistaken about poker, I have already seen some players saying that they were playing well at a certain time because they had made blocks, royals and etc ... In fact the more a player wins without any games in the " arm "as some say, the better this player must be playing.

In supporting software such as Hold'em Manager and Poker Tracker 4, you can see in the graphics how much a player wins or loses chips without showdown, ie without showing the cards. This is REDLINE, the red line on the chart. The alert should sound every time the red line is in a negative projection, as it indicates that the player is giving up a lot, being convinced by the opponent who has a worse game and gives up. On the contrary is the lucrative form of poker, the REDLINE at least stabilized near zero to zero or slightly rising would be the best result. Every time the player can make the opponent drop the pot and the chips, the red line goes up.

In the following chart REDLINE is positive, best scenario possible.

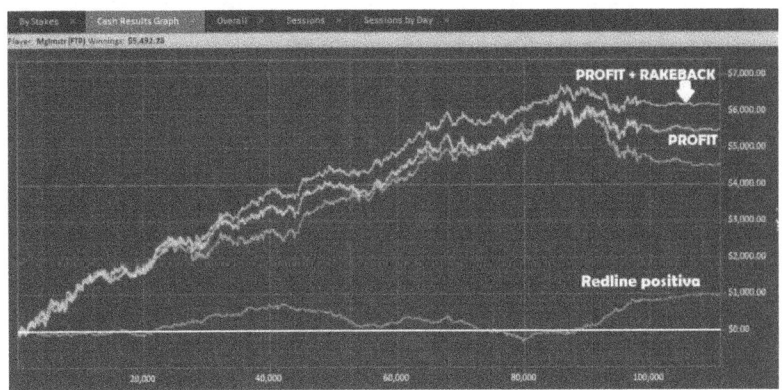

In the graph below, REDLINE is negative and negative projected, this may indicate that the player needs to adjust his game, even with some profit on showdown hands, in which case he is winning a lot of pots on the river by showing the cards and Having the best game.

CHAPTER 7

STARTING THE GAME ...

Hold'em is probably the best known and most popular form of poker today.

Each player starts with two hole cards.

There are three rounds of community cards. These are dealt face up for each player to use, with bets after each round. Players make the best 5-card hand using any combination of the five community cards and two hole cards.

Each new hand starts with a small blind, a big blind and a betting round. Betting rules vary depending on whether the game is Limit, Pot Limit or No Limit.

When the first round of betting is complete, the dealer places the first three community cards, or " the flop ". There is a betting round.

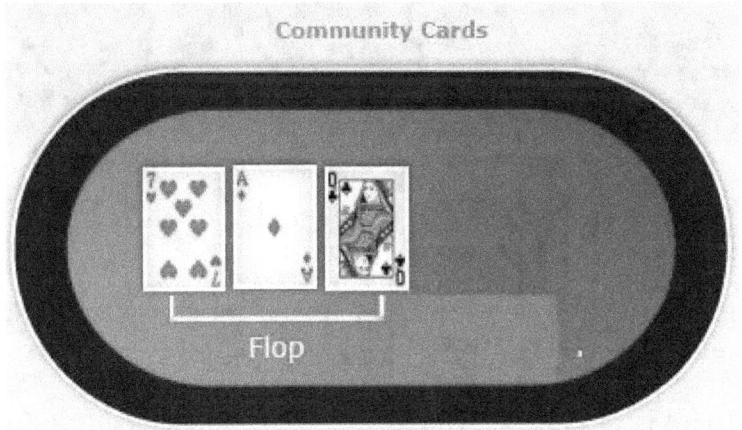

The dealer then places the fourth community card or " the turn ".

There is a betting round. The dealer then places the fifth community card or " the river ".

There is a final round of betting. After the last betting round, the pot is awarded to the best hand.

All Hold'em games include a small blind and big blind. These are forced bets and are determined by the position of the button. These bets are considered live, and all players in the hand must call the big blind, raise or fold.

The button moves clockwise around the table, giving each player a turn being the button, small blind and big blind.

Note: in the following example, the value of 100 chips was placed, BIG BLIND bet , and SMALL BLIND always half or half mandatory bet. The value of 100 chips is fictitious, each game mode, such as tournaments or single table will have the stipulated values, and in tournaments, the value of BIG BLIND, will rise, determined by minutes, ie can start the tournament in 10 and finish after hours in 100,000, because in tournament players will collect chips from each other and increase their stack stacks, if the amount does not increase, the payout would not stimulate the game and could take a long time to finish a tournament. . This is why the phrase " the player was pressured by the increase of blinds to play, would otherwise be swallowed by them ".

At any given time all players start paying the " ANTE ", usually being 10% of the BIG BLIND .

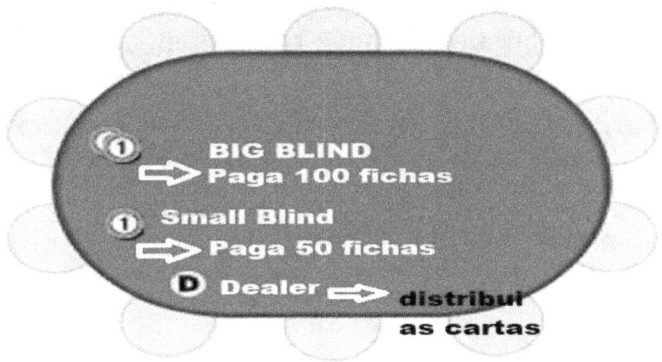

One of the strategies of poker is to avoid entering the play for only the minimum bet, and to avoid this mistake you must raise the stakes with the minimum value being the value of BIG BLIND . In the example above, let's say that a particular player who wants to participate in the play should bet 200 chips, which would be double the amount of BIG BLIND . Recalling that such a raise would already have 350 chips in the pot, 100 from BIG BLIND , 50 from SMALL BLIND and 200 from the raise with a third player.

Here are some general guidelines for hand cards. They are not firm but can give you something to pass up. Of course, the (S) means suitable.

The strongest starting hands:

HIGH PAIR - AA, KK, QQ, JJ, TT (letter 10 is represented by the letter "T")

ACE & HIGH LETTER - SUITES - AKs, AQs, AJs, A10s

NOTE: The letter "s" in the representation means that they are cards of the same suit and "o" (offsuit), different suits. When you already have two suited cards in hand, the chance of forming a FLUSH (5 cards of the same suit) is higher, as you only need to turn 3 of the 5 community cards.

FACES suits - KQs, KJs, QJs

AS and King - AK

Medium hand cards:

KTs, KTo, QTs, QTo, JTs (these types of hands have some chance of forming a sequence from T (10) to As.

MEDIUM COUPLE - (99, 88, 77) - **ATTENTION FOR THESE COUPLES !** There is a basic rule for beginner players: when you are out with middle pairs, if you do not already flop, (the first 3 community cards) the best thing for a beginner player is not to invest too many chips in the pot.

More experienced players take advantage of this foundation by playing other hands in the course of play, in other words, if they do not crack, they often try and manage to play another hand and end up collecting chips, causing opponents to fold.

For novice players, the same rule applies for low pairs as: 22 - 33 - 44 onwards.

TWO HIGH CARDS - AQ, AJ, A10 (Ace King Above, Above), KQ through J10

AS and MEDIUM SUITED - A9 (S), A8 (S), A7 (S)

MEDIUM CONNECTORS SUITED- (No Interval / One Interval) - J9 (S), 109 (S), 108 (S), 98 (S), 97 (S) to 75 (S)

Other Conditional Starting Hands:

NETWORKS - 66, 55, 44, 33, 22 of

ACE and suitable LOW - A6 (S), A5 (S), A4 (S), A3 (S), A2 (S) of the same suit LOW (No gap / one gap) - 65 (S), 64 (S), 54 (S)) 53 (S) (smallest)

7 .1 The position, basic principle

Taking a step forward in our content, we cannot pass up some concepts about POSITION . All poker moves and strategies depend on which position is played, a player positioned better than his opponent speaks last.

A tip for novice players is to avoid playing out of position, unless there is a need, many beginner players make this failure, often losing all of their chips playing out of position unnecessarily.

POSITION is simply where you are sitting relative to the dealer button. In hold em and many other poker games, your position at the table is a big factor. The strength of your position comes from the fact that bets are placed clockwise.

In a favorable position, you can see how many other players react to your hands and whether they fold, bet or call before you. The poker phrase, "Position is power," comes from this simple idea.

There are many names associated with position to identify where players are sitting in relation to the dealer button. Each particular position has its own strengths or weaknesses.

The player to the left of the dealer is not only the small blind but must act first after the flop.

The player to the left of the small blind is the big blind. He or she is already forced to play and is in another starting position after the flop.

The player to the left of the big blind is " under the gun ", also known as " UTG ". This player is the first to act preflop and is considered in the worst position, even if he does not act first in any other round of betting (the blinds) because they would have to invest an entire bet to get in on the action.

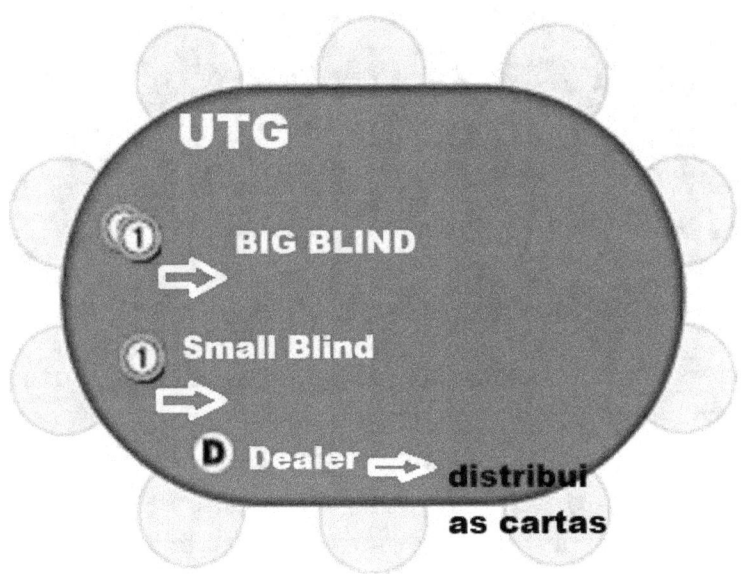

The player with the dealer button is the last to act after the flop and has the most advantageous position. They are called "the dealer", "the button" or just "the button".

The player to the right of the button is called "the CUT off", which comes from the fact that this position is one of the best for blind stealing at a table full of nine or ten hands. This player usually cuts the dealer by betting before he has a chance to bet.

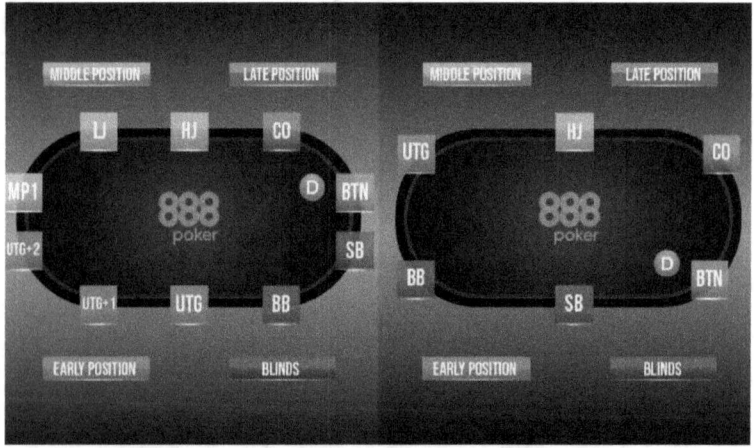

Players in all positions are referred to as starting, intermediate or delayed. Players in an early position are the first to act in a betting round (such as the player under the gun) and players in late position (such as the cutoff and the button) are some of the last to act.

The importance of your position varies on many factors. For example, in no limit hold'em position is much more important than in limit hold'em. It is always better to be in a late position, so it is important to identify what hands are generally playable in all positions.

Let's say you are under the gun. You have inappropriate Queen-Ten and decide to enter the pot. The player who bets after you raise, and all but you fold. Now you are in a jam. Chances are good that this player has a better hand than you. If they have an ace pair, king or pair, they are statistically better than you.

You would suspect that someone you created has at least one such hand. You can now call again or flop like an underdog or you can fold and fold. Worse, if you call, you will be acting before this player for the rest of the hand.

On the other hand, let's say you're on the button. You have the inadequate Queen-Ten and everyone bends to you. One option would be to give up and let the blinds fight. Another would be the fair call and see what happens on the flop. Many players here would raise because you could steal the blinds and even if you didn't, you would act behind them for the rest of the hand. Raising is only a viable option because of its favorable position.

Another notable factor is that the position goes hand in hand with the knowledge of the players directly around you. For example, an aggressive player who steals the blinds to a tight player's immediate right usually results in theft of the tight player's blinds.

Being in late position with a good hand has great strengths compared to early with a good hand. Early position raisers assume a good hand and tend to push players away.

The initial preflop raises strength opponents to make two bets at the same time - a minimum in the event of no limit - with nothing in the pot yet. In late position there may be players who have already called a bet. These players only need to call a (limit) bet with a little something already in the pot. Thus, late position players with a good hand have the ability to manipulate the pot.

While position is important, you also need to calculate the best odds of getting the card you need to win. We call these advantages and disadvantages.

REMEMBER IF:

The position factor will be present in all betting, preflop, flop, turn and river rounds. So if you get involved in an out-of-position play (such as when a player is in a worse position than your opponent), you will have to deal with it until the end of the play.

The following is a practical example of what position means in poker.

We are at a table with 9 players, a player in position 3 gets in the worst possible way, only calling the blind, 800 chips.

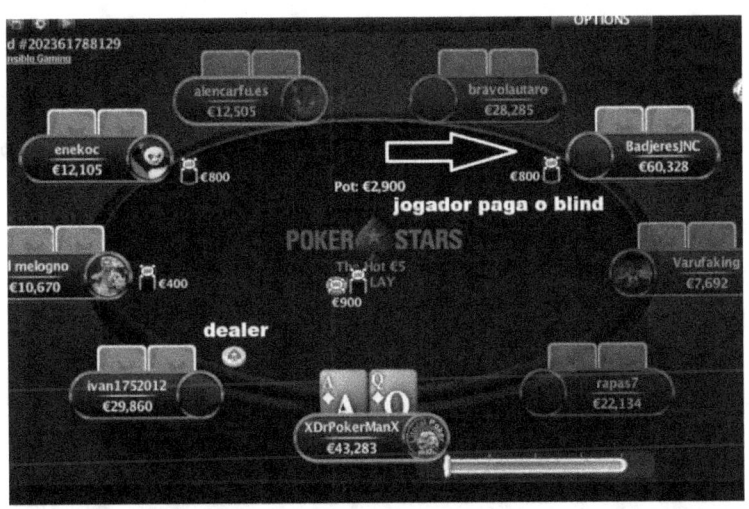

Me, "XDrPokerManX", I'm in a position before the best, "Dealer". If I raise to 2,280 chips, the amount to be raised may vary, being recommended about 3x the value of the blind plus 1 blind for each opponent in the play, in this case it would be about 3x 800 = 2,400 + 800 (1 blind (already had a player in hand), would be a value of 3,200. Now comes the question: the recommended would be 3,200, but XDrPokerManX increased by 2,280 for what reason? The rule is usually recommended for beginner players who usually do not know how much to raise, since raising too little attracts many players into the pot, and raising too much amazes all players and no more chips are won. As novice players said, I have to say how much I don't want novice players to learn to play poker systematically, as in most poker books and manuals I've seen since I started playing poker in mid-2009. Less information back then, we have a lot more content on the internet today and we can accelerate learning. With that in mind, I will introduce more sophisticated moves even to new players in this book.

Continuing, I raised to 2,280 chips in the expectation that only the player who had only paid 800 would get into the hand, or in the worst case scenario, another player, such as the dealer, had the best possible position right after me.

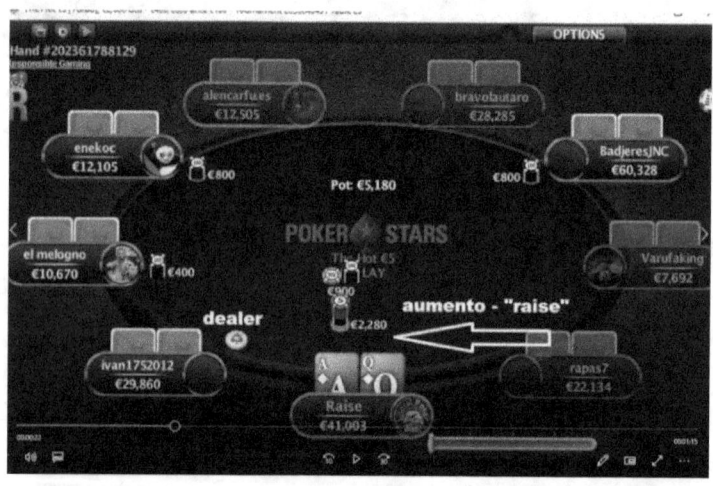

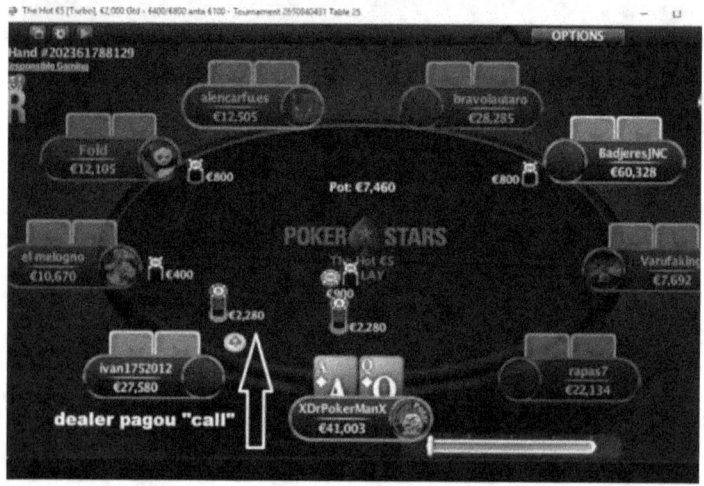

My plan worked, the dealer only paid 2,280 and the player who only paid 800 only completed 2,280. In different situations, when this player who had only paid 800, on his turn to raise, should be careful, depending on the opponent's profile, compensates until giving up, as some players will only limp to take a raise. and then raise to make a giant pot by having a "premium" hand like an AA or KK.

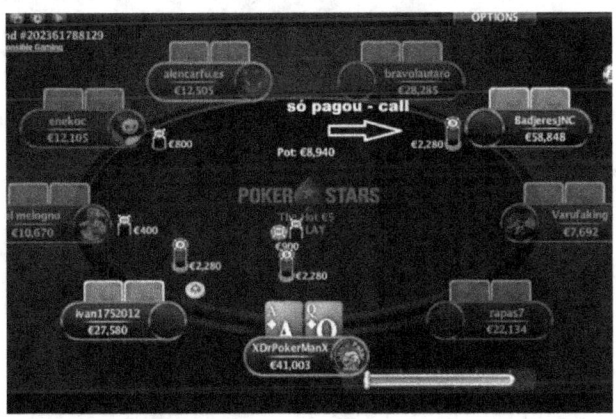

But in my case this player just called and we flopped with him and the dealer.

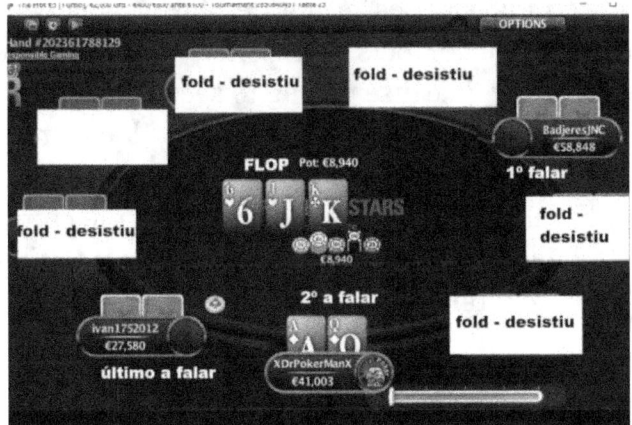

In this example, "XDrPokerManX" has a better position than "BadjeresJNC", but worse position with respect to dealer "ivan1752012".

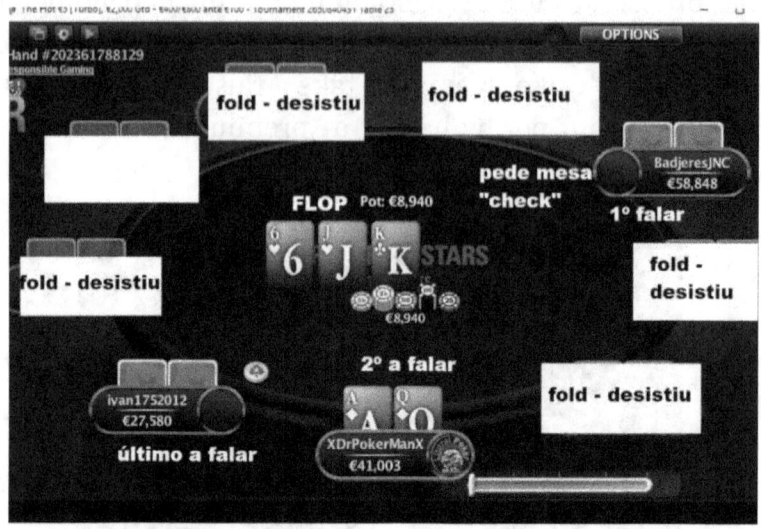

The first player checks, and "XDrPokerManX" missed anything, just waits for a T (ten) to make a straight, and still has the dealer talking after him. As I said, this example is sophisticated and I will show you what an experienced player does. A novice player usually checks, too, so if the dealer bets, everyone should fold without hitting anything, because paying to see if they hit the turn is not a profitable move in the long run. So, XDrPokerManX bets about 40% of the pot value, in an attempt to make opponents fold and leave the chips, or at worst, the dealer folds (which is in a better position) and only the player stands. that was in a worse position.

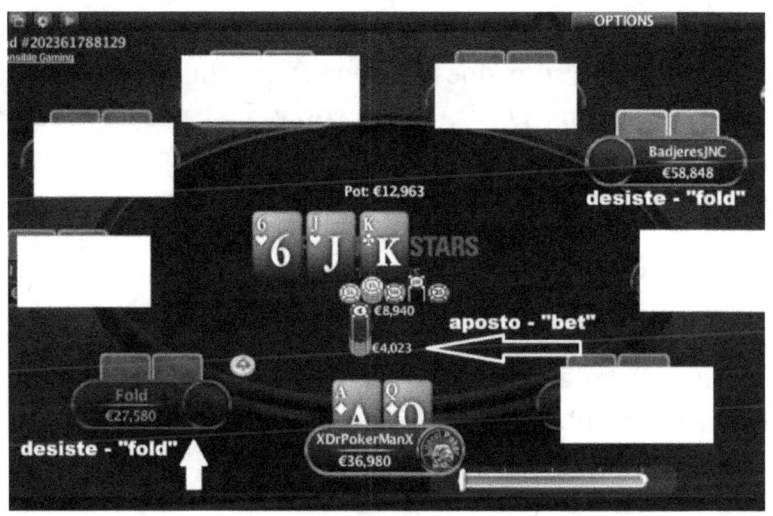

In the example, both opponents folded and XDrPokerManX won the pot with 8,940 chips.

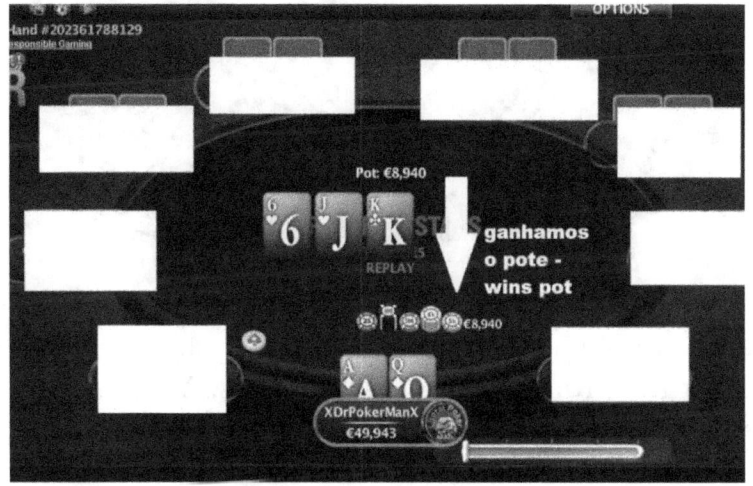

It is important to mention that in cases like this, it is interesting that the winner does not show the cards, as it is good that the opponents believe that he hit a high pair at least. The profit in poker comes from these moves where the winner accumulates chips without reaching the river last card, so it doesn't depend on the luck factor to win. If you don't get it, don't worry, just pin down how important it is to have a better position than your opponent so you can always talk last in betting rounds.

7 .2 Playing FLOP

In addition to the handling of the pocket cards, and your decision to fold or hold them, the flop is probably the most important moment in Texas Hold 'em.

Three cards hit the board, often causing "worthless" hands to come out of weak cards and sometimes rendering strong pocket cards useless. Your ability to read the flop will be a big factor in your success in Texas Hold 'em.

Flopping 3 of a Kind

There is a difference between flopping a set and flopping trips. First, flopping a set would be a situation where you have a strong pair, like KK, and the river comes with KA-6. Your monster 3 Kings is hidden, and anyone with an Ace will probably be raising, seeing top pair on the flop. The potential for this hand is incredible, and slow play would be a good option.

A similar situation, let's call flopping trips. This would be a situation where you only have one of three cards as a pocket letter. Let's say you hold AK suited and the flop comes out KKQ.

Here again, you have 3 of a kind, but you still have to understand that this is a little weaker. Whenever a pair is displayed on board, there is danger of a full house already formed.

QQ would definitely be a hand someone would hold, and if you get this flop, your 3 Kings are losers. It is also harder to maximize a pot with both kings on the flop. These are huge scare cards, and if you bet right away, you can get nothing more than what is already in the pot. Again, play slowly and be especially careful with a full house already formed.

There are, however, certain times that you want to tie the pot with 3 of a kind. If the flop gives chances for a straight draw, such as KK-10, where anyone with QJ has a good straight chance, or if 2 of the cards are of the same suit, giving someone the chance of a flush if they hold one. Pair of cards of the same suit. In such cases, they will play on the river, so pay to see extra cards!

Another time you want to tie the pot is if you flopped a small set. For example, you checked with the big blind with a pair of 3 and the flop came Q-8-3. You have your set, and you'll probably win with it, but you don't want to risk someone holding a higher pair by getting your set on the turn or river for free. Bet, raise, check raise if you know someone will bet, what you have to do to slow your competition and hopefully push the middle pairs. What you like to see is someone with AQ in this situation with top pair, top kicker who will give you action but has little chance of winning. Jam the pot with small sets.

Top pair after the flop

If you have a high pair before the flop and are drawing the pot then you should continue with the pot if you still have the top pair. If you have QQ and the flop comes out 10-2-7, you're probably still the leader unless someone is slow playing Ace or Kings before the flop, or someone with 10 just flopped a set.

The fact is, if you play aggressively with a high pair before the flop, you will usually know whether or not you still have the lead.

If you have AK, and the flop comes 4-K-9, here again, you are playing the pot. You have a top pair with the best kicker, and the last thing you want is for someone to come out and complete a flush or straight to defeat you.

Top pair is strong after the flop, but definitely not strong enough to sit and play slowly.

Flopping a small pair

Suppose you had A-8 of clubs and the flop was Q-8-3. You lost your flush draw, because only the 3 are clubs, but you made a pair of "babies" on the flop. You have to respect the fact that someone can have a queen and have to win. Even so, if the action is scheduled for you, you should seriously consider placing a bet here. By betting, you accomplish the purpose of discovering the true strength of your partner. If anyone has a queen, you can expect a raise. If you have a high hand, expect calls. If you are raised then you must consider the personality of who raised you. If a weak or tough player raises you, then it may be time to call or give up. If you are the mediocre player then stay and even re-raise.

This particular hand can be hard to fold simply because you still have a lot of outs. An ace would give you a huge hand; 8 more would be even better, and there is always the possibility of 2 more clubs hitting the board.

So go ahead and bet on the small pairs, and then judge for your personalities and sufficient actions as to where you are.

Flopping a monster

By monster hand we mean to flop a royal flush, 4 of a kind, full house, flush, straight and straight flush. Statistically the hand is yours or practically yours. In most circumstances, the best option is to slow down the game. You want the other players to stand and build a decent hand that they will bet with or at least call the river.

We offer a word of caution though. In the case of flushes and straights, be sure not to get caught with the low end of a straight or low flush, where someone makes the same straight with a higher card, or someone flushes the same with a higher card. .

If you are playing good quality pocket cards, this should rarely happen. But if your flush is only 10, make an aggressive bet and try to drive anyone with a jack, queen, king or ace from your suit. Granted, most people won't fold four to a flush, but at least you're making them pay for a chance to get their card.

As a general rule, then, slowly play the monsters and wait until the most expensive turn and river to start extracting chips from your opponents.

Flopping Flush or Straight Draw

You have to first understand that the odds are still against you by making your hand (2-1 with four to one flush or open ended). But the general rule to follow is that Texas Hold'em rewards aggressive play. Bet this hand if it is marked for you and wait for one of two results. Either everyone else folds and you take a small pot, or you flush or straight and win a big one.

If there are bets and raises for you, you will need to resort to calculating the pot odds to determine if it is profitable to make a call or, in some cases, to raise.

Flopping 2 Pairs

Let's say you hold J-10 suited, and the flop comes out 10-4-J. You managed to flop the first two pairs. I would tend to fill the pot with two pairs. While two pairs are strong, there are still many hands that can beat him. It's okay to roll the pot and elbow everyone off the table. If you end up doing a full house on the back streets, you can adjust your strategy, but for a moment you want to bet and force the limpers.

There are exceptions to this, of course. If you hold AQ and the flop comes out AQ2, you are very strong and can let someone catch a little. Read the texture of the flop. If the flop is suited or connected, you definitely do not want to mess with slow play, but rather place your chips while you are in front and call the draw hands to play. Flops that show little help to other players may be worth playing a bit so that they improve well enough to place their bets on the turn and river or give an aggressive player a chance to bluff.

Flopping Trash

If you are holding a marginal hand, and it is not helped at all by the flop, plan to check and fold. Bringing bad hands to the river will have a big impact on your bankroll.

You can hear the cha-ching in your ears as you bet those good hands. However, for the beginner, this street can be exceptionally dangerous, as this is where many players complete their straight and flush, along with all the other poker possibilities.

If you have played good poker up to this point, both in card selection and on the flop, then you may have some idea whether or not you are in the hand. As a general rule, if you are in front after seeing this 4th card hit the board, bet and start building the pot. On the other hand, if you are sure that you are behind, this is the prime time to fold your hand before you start throwing your money away by paying the most expensive bets.

Let's say you got JJ and bet aggressively before and after the flop. The flop and turn board look like this: Q-3-7-A, three of which are diamonds and unfortunately you hold black jacks (spades and clubs). You must double this hand for any raise. Why? Count how many ways you are defeated: an ace, a queen, two or a diamond if another appears on the river, plus a remote opportunity if the river card is 10, K or another Jack. That is a lot of ways to hit you.

Now count how many outs you have and the best possible hand you can make. Now your best hope is another Jack, giving you three of a kind. Are you willing to place bets and raises when there are only two cards left in the deck that can help you, and yet you still have a chance of being beaten by someone blessed with a diamond or straight flush?

Good pre- and post-flop poker plays give you the information you need to make the decision on the turn. Stay with your instinct. If you are ahead, bet and if you are behind, fold unless you are getting good pot odds with a draw hand. Do not pray for miraculous cards. Play the cards you hold.

Now that you have the flop, the turn will come, but perhaps the most significant card you want to see is the river.

7.3 Playing the Turn

This is perhaps the most important place in the Texas Holdem poker game because it is a very important decision moment, a decision that can bring you a lot of chips in the long run. This is where a good chunk of chips is extracted from opponents still dreaming of hitting their River card!

Remember that raising the pot from the preflop is critical to making sense of this line of thinking, but always being careful not to compromise all of your chips so far.

This is also a time to decide to fold, since if your opponent has dueled you preflop and flop, he may actually be beating you, so it could be a moment of reflection, and one more reason to bet before, because If you do not bet or raise, you will not have information about the villain's interest in the pot.

7 . 4 Playing the River

The River Showdown Card It's time to see who is taking the chips, and who is drowning in the river. The game on the river is quite simple. If you have the best hand, either by good card strength at the beginning or river luck, now is your last chance to get a few more chips from your opponents.

Some "classic" players will check here, even though they know they have the best hand and thus save a few dollars for their opponents to put back in their wallets. Unless you are a longtime friend, I would advise taking your wallet, emptying it of its contents, and then sticking the wallet in his throat. There are winners and losers in poker. If you are looking for "courtesy play" then play with the family. The poker world is like the icy terrain of Jack London, where only the strong survive.

The only real advice we can give about river play is almost never to give up. If you have played good cards up to this point of the hand, then you have at least one chance to hold the winning cards. So far, the pot is big enough that you also have a good sense of money to stay at home.

Unless you have not completed a pure draw, make any bet. Don't get the reputation of someone who can be banished from the river. If this happens, you will only face more and more bluffs on the river. On the other hand, if you get the reputation of someone who can't be bluffed, no one in their right mind will tempt you.

The only other times you should think about folding is when an extremely conservative non-bluffing player is calling a whole draw hand and now it looks like he has hit his card.

Or when there are two or more players starting to bet and raise on the river, you can be sure that at least one of them holds the goods. You can make a case to fold here.

Pot odds dictate that you bet or call on the river unless you are pretty sure that you have won.

7 . 5 The reason for betting

No one is always a winner, and anyone who says he is, is a liar or does not play poker.

A bet is a statement that:

a) "I have the best hand and I'll bet money on it" or

b) "You have a weak hand and you will fold if you are forced to bet on it"

Normally, players should bet when they have a good hand. Players who do not have good hands should fold. Of course, if it were that simple, there would be no need for this book.

You can bet on Tic-Tac-Toe. Most players play against this idea by trying to be a shrewd or deceptive player. Don't fall into this trap when you are just learning to play.

Your betting strategy should be built on this simple idea, but you should know when to deviate and bet in situations you would not otherwise do. Here are some situations you should start looking to improve your game:

Blind Theft

When you are in the dealer position, and only you and the blinds remain in the game, a raise is often called a "blind-steal". This is because the blinds may fold, whereas if you didn't raise but simply called, the blinds would simply check. It's a good way to make a buck or two, but it will never make you rich. It's another way to end the game fast and have a new hand with more players (and more money).

The Rising Theft - Re-Steal

If you are the last to act and all players have checked for you, betting to simply limit the number of players or take the pot is called stealing. Do not use this exclusively, as better players will come to you quickly and start checking against your (worst) bad hand.

It's good to use a steal raise when you have an excellent draw hand, such as a nut flush draw. Players will tend to "check to the raiser". If you take your hand, you now have a bigger pot to win. If you don't, you can always check and wait for the fifth card to make your hand.

Fold Equity

Although not correct, many players get into a poker hand in order to hit a big game, an aces court, a royal flush and other winning combinations. In the course of the book, we have mentioned several times that in order to achieve long-term profitability in poker, one must win chips by making opponents fold to collect the chips in play. Being the only way to make the "villain" run is by betting, and even when you have a hand with any chance of forming a winning game, betting or raising still has what we call "fold equity" or "fold equity". , which is one more chance to win the pot by folding, that is, when betting on a fair hand, we have a double chance of getting it right if our game comes in or the villain folds.

CHAPTER 8

INSERTING PROFIT STRATEGIES IN YOUR GAME

8 .1 How to play postflop on tables with many limpers

When you see a lot of preflop calls and almost no check-raises, thank heaven because it indicates that your table is full of loose-passive players.

Before the flop, the best way to take advantage of this limping festival is to fire higher than standard raises, preferably when you have position. The idea is to find out how willing they are to call these raises with speculative hands. "Far more often than they should" is the answer we usually find.

Let's say you're at a no-limit hold'em table with $ 1- $ 2 blinds. Two loose-passive opponents limp, you have position and shoot $ 20, both call. Just by the preflop action, this is already a lucrative move. But, from now on, how should we act? Let's look at the best way to play this postflop hand.

Sometimes you will get a high pair or hit a strong hand on the flop. In such cases, you are almost certain to pull the pot regardless of how you play. Therefore, we will not worry about these situations for now. Instead, let's assume you were dealt a marginal hand and the flop was not so great for you. In exchange for kids, although you may have the best hand, you would be happy to take the chips without dispute.

If one of the loose-passive counterattacks you, the chance that it is a pure bluff is practically zero. Players like that simply don't bluff against the preflop raiser. The only question you should ask is if he could be betting with a draw or something with a weak pair. If the answer is yes, then you can have the best hand - or calling without anything can be of some value.

However, the only reason to draw this conclusion is that you have seen this opponent bet a few times with marginal hands. If this is the case, there is probably some value in calling the flop. Unless it improves on the turn, a loose-passive player will fold after that street, or weakly take the initiative with a second bet, often similar in size to the flop bet. As a strong and aggressive player, you should be able to sense his weakness and take the pot on the turn or river. You won't always succeed, but your aggression must work often enough for the flop call to be a profitable move.

On the other hand, if loose-passive flop bets are usually legitimate, it is better to simply fold and wait for the next hand. Often trying to force you to quit is throwing money away. Some think it 's a big sign of weakness to raise $ 20 preflop and then fold before a flop bet, but that's just the ego speaking. Just thank him because, as loose-passive, he gave you a hint about the strength of his hand before you had invested even more chips. A more treacherous player would have allowed you to make a continuation bet, and then check raise.

You should not face a loose-passive bet very often. They will usually check before you on the flop, at which point you should bet. But don't allow yourself to overdo it. It is worth avoiding the common mistake of betting too much on the flop against this type of opponent.

Before the flop, our goal was to test the upper limits of loose-passives. What is the biggest raise they would be willing to call? Postflop, we want to test your lower limits. And if they didn't hit the flop, what will happen most of the time? How small can our bet be for them to fold? Players like this usually do not pay attention to pot odds, betting size, or placing their opponents in a range of hands. Instead, they just want to know if they hit the flop or not.

Let's say you get something like Q ♥ 9 ♥ and the flop comes 7 ♣ 4 ♦ 2 ♠ . If you bet $ 20 into a $ 60 pot, their initial instinct is not to think, "I have 4-to-1 on the call and two overcards, and he may be betting for nothing." They also overlook the fact that hitting a queen or a nine can give them the best hand. They also don't realize that even if they don't get it right, you can check on the turn, and maybe fold the river in front of a bluff.

Trust me, this is not the thinking of a typical loose-passive player. In fact, his head must be passing something like, "Damn, I didn't hit anything on this flop. I'm not going to spend another $ 20 on that hand. "

On the contrary, if he hits hard enough, he will call. That simple. In most cases, the size of your bet will not influence his decision. Moreover, given that they are passive, they will rarely check raise. Putting it all together, why make a pot-size bet when a 1/3 will have the same results?

Earlier in the article, I said that the size of our preflop raise should sometimes be larger than standard, defying common sense. No book will tell you to raise the big blind 10 times after two limps, as constantly you will only get action from hands that beat you. However, when it comes to a limping festival at a cheap no-limit hold'em table, this logic almost never applies. Some players will simply call high raises with very speculative hands.

However, some of them will play the "hit or drop" style on the flop, in which case it will not be difficult to get them out of hand. Betting $ 20 into a $ 60 pot, hoping to fold opponents, may seem an even bigger challenge to common sense than preflop raising. Against the right opponents, however, is clearly the correct move.

Whether you bet $ 20 or $ 60, they will fold with the hands that you missed, and pay with the hands you connected. Therefore, there is no reason to wager more than necessary. The idea is to find the minimum bet size that will give you the information you need about their hand.

But beware: Not all loose-passive players are the same. Many of them have different calling patterns and will react differently to your bets and raises. Next month, we'll dig deeper into this, and discuss what to do when the hand reaches the turn and river. ♠

Matt Lessinger is the author of The Book of Bluffs: How to Bluff and Win at Poker, available everywhere. You can find Matt's other articles at www.CardPlayer.com.

8.2 Paying in Attack Position by Floating

When we play poker for many years, it is easy to forget that the technical language of the game can be quite different from the traditional language, especially for us whose language is Portuguese. If you don't read enough or are new to the game, some concepts may be unfamiliar or beat. What are implied reverse odds? What is stack to pot ratio? To remind you or help you not to get lost in a professional conversation, we bring you this column: "Explaining Poker Like I Had Five". In each issue, a new concept or term - and you're likely to always come across one or two of them in the middle of our articles.

THE CONCEPT: FLOATING

It consists of calling a bet or raise with the intention of winning the pot by bluffing on later streets. Good players often float to show strength but without having to inflate the pot by raising.

Floating is simply calling with a hand that has little (or no equity) to bluff on the turn or river.

GIVE ME AN EXAMPLE

One player raises from the middle of the table and you call with 6 ♠ 5 ♠ . The blinds fold and you see the flo p J ♦ J ♥ 9 ♥ . Your opponent makes a half-pot continuation bet.

At this point your hand has no value. You could fold and move to the next hand. However, you have already noticed that your opponent always makes a continuation bet when he raises preflop. So there is a good chance that he completely missed the flop.

You want this pot for yourself, but a raise would make the pot too big if the opponent called - and with your hand, that is the last thing you want. You then go to the float and just call to see what he will do on the turn.

The turn is a 2 ♠ . Your opponent checks. You bet half the pot and he folds. Maybe he dropped a middle pair or AK. Either way, your float allowed you to take the pot with the worst hand and pay a cheap price.

Of course, sometimes things don't go as we planned. Let's say on the same turn, your opponent bets again. Well, the odds of him having a hand now increased. The best thing you can do is throw your cards away and forget about the chips that were sacrificed on the flop. Or the turn brought a K ♥ , and he kept betting. By not raising the flop, you may have given your opponent the chance to hit the King. And there are still cases where you will bet the flop and your opponent will raise, causing you to lose not only the flop bet but also the bet. turn

Floating is an advanced move that should be added to your arsenal, but use it wisely: in position against predictable players who tend to play their weak or medium hands passively after the flop. ♠

CardPlayer Team

https://cardplayer.com.br/revistas/98/explicando-poker-como-se-eu-tivesse-cinco-floating/2284

8 .3 Different Ways to Play Low Pairs Profitably

In this subchapter, three professional players wrote to CardPlayer Brasil about how to play low pairs in the mid and late tournament stages when you have medium stacks - a very common situation, but that can still raise some doubts.

Fabiano Kovalski

Santa Catarina, specialist in Multi-Table Tournaments online. In 2010, he made two BSOP final tables and has amassed over $ 800,000 in prizes.

Vitor Brasil

Carioca participated in the MTT Pro project in 2010 and was one of the first chosen for the Poker Villa Project. Has over $ 300,000 in awards.

Felipe Nunes

Catarinense, participated in the Sng Team Pro, reaching the goal of $ 10,000 in just one month and two days. Already has nearly $ 800,000 in career awards.

How do you play low pairs (2-2 to 6-6) in the middle and final stages of tournaments with not so comfortable stacks, between 15 and 25 big blinds?

Fabiano Kovalski: In blinds, pairs generally have a great deal of equity against any range. So whenever I am in the blinds and someone attacks me, I have an ideal re-steal situation, ie when someone in late position raises I go all-in. If action comes in GAP, I evaluate the villain's aggression in the big blind, and choose to go all-in straight, raise / call or even raise / fold in the case of a weak opponent. If I am among the last to speak, I play as in the small blind, altering my plan according to the aggressiveness of the opponents. If I'm in the starting position, I usually open fold. At this stage, I preserve my stack for re-steals in the blinds.

Felipe Nunes: With stacks in this range, low pairs become good for steal and re-steal. At this stage they are usually great for late position play. However, be careful, as many good players overestimate the value of the low pairs and end up in high variance situations, just because the fairness of these pairs at the showdown is usually good. They really gain strength when you're in the blinds, as you can often just call and play for set value, or steal and re-steal any opponent who is abusing the position. I think it is totally quiet to call the blinds a normal bet from any position on the table and to play for set value, even with a stack of around 20 big blinds.

Vitor Brasil: In blind warfare situations, if I'm in the big blind, I almost always play aggressively. With 15 to 20 blinds I re-steal / all-in with any pair. In case the small blind completes, I shove. With 25 big blinds, I'm going to re-steal / shove. If the villain completes in the small blind, raise the bet to 3.5 to 4 times the blind. In the small blind, with the action coming in GAP, I always go all-in. With GAP in the other positions, I fold and save my stack for re-steal. On the cut off and the button, I push in with 20 big blinds or less. Up to 25 big blinds, I raise between 2.3 and 2.5 times the blind. Limped pots are less likely then, and should be analyzed separately. Against a villain who gives a lot of limps, it's easier to shove with any pair. As for a villain who doesn't limp often, only pairs over six are good to push, as the opponent's range is suited connectors and smaller pairs.

♠

What is the best approach when playing low pairs at the beginning of deep stack tournaments?

Fabiano Kovalski: Playing low pairs in deep tournaments (over 100 big blinds) is quite simple. Basically, game for set value. If I miss the flop, I fold and fold to the next hand. In unopened pots, I usually raise to build a big pot. So when I hit a set, I extract more value and make it harder for my opponents to read.

Felipe Nunes: In tournaments like this, I try to play with hands that generate great value when they hit the board. I'm not after top pair or overpair. So low pairs fit perfectly into deep tournaments, because when I hit the set I have a hand that is hard to read and wreaks havoc on opponents' stacks. But not only is the poker player worth living, so when you have position you should play aggressively to get postflop action. Without position, the task is easier because most of the time, it's just set value, so post-flop decisions end up being simple. In this case, I just prefer to call my opponents raise - except when the table folds and I'm in the small blind: then I raise with any pair.

Vitor Brasil: In pots not yet opened, I always raise. They vary and can reach 4 big blinds if the tournament is deep. In pots with many limpers, raise to try to isolate the hand. In a situation of five or more limpers, I also limp. In raised and reraised pots I fold, because the player who opened the pot can raise again; In this case, playing for set value is not profitable. In increased pots, the options are varied: the tighter the opponent, the more prone to call, since the villain's range is very small and I have a good chance of getting his whole stack up when I hit the set. Against a very aggressive player the call becomes marginal as there are rare times when you can get the whole stack out of it. If the pot is played by three or more people, the call becomes interesting. Remember that position here has its influence, but not so much, since small pairs are the worst hands to try to bluff, float or the like. With just two outs, hand equity is not so good

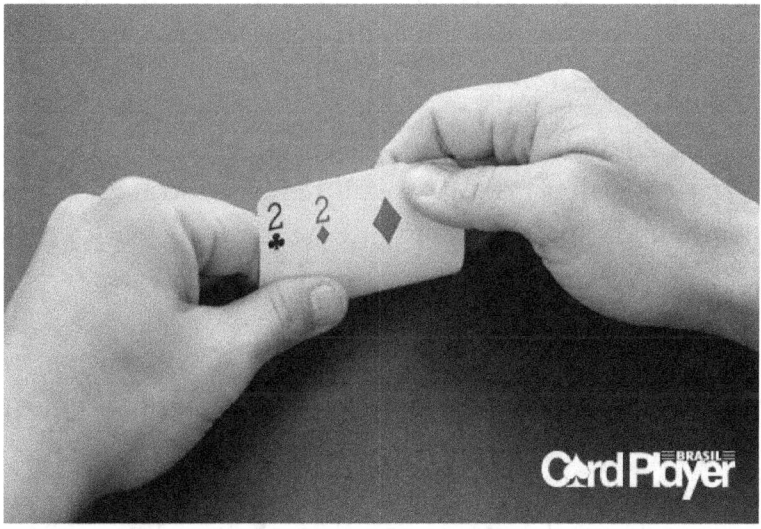

https://cardplayer.com.br/revistas/43/mental-games-how-playing-pares-baixos-on-tourners/1223

8.4 Basic Strategies for Your Chip Stack

Playing Short Stack

This is the 10th article I write for CardPlayer Brazil and I am very proud of it. I confess that when I received the invitation of Marcelo Souza, editor of the magazine, I did not have a definite plan for the sequence of themes and I saw it as an exercise in systematizing and describing the theoretical and practical knowledge that I acquired in those years as a professional poker player. At the same time, it's been a challenge for me, I mean, to bring it in an accessible way at all levels, deepening just what is needed to help novice players - and some middlemen - better understand the concepts and operation of the game and consequently improve their level. Today I can say that the experiment was successful, both in terms of the production of the texts and in support of the readers. It encourages me to continue.

To commemorate the ten articles, I am releasing a series of three texts that briefly explain the basic strategies and fundamentals for each stack range, starting with short stacks. After all, tournaments are, above all, stack games.

Short Stack Strategies

We consider a short stack that up to 20 big blinds. This is the stack range where we have the least space for postflop play, leading the vast majority of pots to be decided preflop, taking advantage of the remaining fold equity. It is very common to find ourselves in these situations on tournament straights where mistakes cost a lot more.

The classic short-stack game manual suggests the following:

Stacks up to 10 bbs: critical situation. There is no room for anything but push or all-in.

Stacks between 12 and 15 bbs: warning signal on. We should not waste chips opening raises with weak hands. There is virtually no preflop raise-fold.

Stacks between 16 and 20 bbs: resteal mode. Perfect stack range to exploit who is stealing too much because we still have fold equity, meaning the villain is not committed to the pot when raising and facing a Hero all-in [about resteals, see "Thief" Stealing Thief ", issue 71].

Raise-fold with short stacks

With the constant development of the game, these rules, previously seen as dogmas, were gradually overcome. Does this mean that key concepts like pot odds, fold equity and range analysis have been forgotten? No, quite the contrary, they are being exploited to their limit.

Today, it is accepted that in certain situations with a range consisting mainly of blockers (hands containing cards that "block" the frequency of big hands in action - for example, if we have an ace, we reduce the chance of an ace by 50%. AA from the front), it is possible to mini-raise and fold against a 3-bet or shove (all-in). For example, on a tight table or where there is pressure for prize jumps. The great advantage is that this play is difficult to exploit as there is not enough room for a 3-bet light that does not compromise with the Hero's shove.

3-bet light with 18 to 20 bbs

Another tool adopted by regulars is the 3-bet light with 18 to 20bbs. This is a good strategy for maintaining the stack against very aggressive players. Mathematically, the

Hero is not committed to the pot. Let's look at an example:

Hero at BTN with 20 bbs.

Villain in MP with 40bbs.

Loose-Aggressive Villain (LAG) mini-raises, Hero with A ♦ 5 ♦ on BTN makes a 4.2bbs 3-bet. If the villain goes all-in, the Hero would have to pay 15.8 bbs for a final pot of 42.5 (counting blinds and before). This means that the Hero must have at least 37% equity in order for the call to be break even (no long term profit or loss). Assuming the Villain goes all-in with the following range: 88+, ATs +, AQo +, KQs and KQo (8%); o A ♦ 5 ♦ has only 36.6% equity, that is, it does not have what is necessary even for zero to zero, but only for a call with a positive value expectation.

Since the Hero invests 4.2 bbs with the intention of winning a 8.25 pot, if action ends preflop, 3-bet has to pass only 50% of the time to be a long-term winner on its own. . A villain LAG tends to raise with a frequency of around 30% of hands. If he only reacts to that 8% range, it means that much more than half of the time he raises, he will fold to Hero's 3-bet.

Top mistakes of beginning players

Firstly, it must be made clear that while these new tools are needed in every good player's arsenal, short stacks must still be played tightly. Surgical precision in actions is required as a raise represents a valuable part of the stack. If we have 12 bbs and we raise, we put 16.6% of our stack into play. How many times will we raise-fold until we are in a totally critical situation?

But the worst mistake a player can make is to play passively. Flat calling (just calling a raise) should be avoided as much as possible, especially with marginal hands such as small pairs and suited connectors, as we are very dependent on the texture of the flop and have no room to develop the hand to the river. .

So we wrap up the short-stack subject. In the next installment, I'll cover average stacks, those between 25 and 40 bbs, which is the stack range tournament players are most used to playing - but that's where they make the most mistakes.

Basic Strategies by Stack Range

One student once said to me, "My problem is that I can build a good stack in the beginning, but it gets there midway through the tournament, when we have between 25 and 30 big blinds, I feel very stuck and My stack melts like a flake ice cream on a sunny day. When I realize, I'm in push / fold. " Well, the flake ice cream part, I added myself. But one thing I am sure of: many of the readers identified with the student's speech.

This is the stack range where aggression is most important. Here the arsenal of moves is wider and more complex than in the short stack game. Sitting and waiting for the best hands is far from the right strategy. Good players, even those with tight tendencies, can exploit the situations they present themselves using all the available tools - taking advantage of their image, of course.

In this issue's article, we will discuss the main strategic notions for the medium stack game, that is, between 25 and 40 bbs, quite common in decisive moments of the tournaments.

3-bet and 4-bet Light

Stacks between 25 and 30 bbs are great for 3-bet light. This is because, in general, we leave the opponent with no room to react. Imagine a situation where we have 30 bbs of effective stack. Our opponent raises 2bbs and we 3-bet the button to 5bbs. Now let's look at the opponent's possibilities:

- If he calls, he will have to play postflop out of position. The pot on the flop will be over 10bbs, with 25bbs behind, meaning there is no room for much maneuvering.

- If you 4bet, which will be between 10x and 12x (sizes most commonly used by players), you will be investing 30% to 40% of the stack.

- If all-in, you will have to invest your 30 bbs to win a pot that is at about 9.5 bbs. This is the most common move when a player decides to react within this stack range.

We can conclude that it is very difficult to react to a 3-bet. Calling leads to an unfavorable postflop situation, and 4-bet costs a very large part of the stack. Going all in is the best way to react, but as it may cost the tournament, you need to be extra careful about this move. It is precisely this set of factors that favors the effectiveness of 3-bet light with 30 bbs.

Stacks around 40 bbs are great for 4-bet light. Let's take another example to clarify the idea.

On the button, gapped, and with 40 bbs stack, we raised 2 bbs. The same stacked BB 3-bet to 5 bbs. We apply a 4-bet to 10bbs. What happens?

- if villain calls, you have the old problem of throwing a big pot out of position. The pot will be 20 bbs and the effective stack will be 30 bbs. Nothing to do but twist to hit the flop.

- If the villain opts for 5-bet, it has to be all-in.

It is easy to see how limited the opponent's chances of reacting are.

Set Value and Suited Connectors

About small pairs, I wrote about it earlier [issue 76 or Eiji blog]. So with stacks up to 40 bbs, it will be hard to find a situation where we will have implied good enough odds to play for set value. Also, raising in early and middle positions is not advisable either, as it is a hand that does not offer good chances for postflop play.

The suited connectors have another problem. They give the illusion of being good hands to play postflop in position. However, they do not top pair with a good frequency. When a KX or AX hits a top pair, they have very good flop equity, even against strong ranges, unlike suited connectors, as we will not have postflop space for big maneuvers. But nothing prevents us from using some of these hands in our 3-bet light range, especially in position.

Flat call

You need to have a flat call range with these stacks for final positions and blinds. For this action, hands that make top pair and / or draw are good . One thing is to have a flush draw with 7 ♦ 6 ♦ on the flop T ♦ 2 ♦ 3 ♠ . Another is to have with K ♦ Q ♦ .

The flat call range I suggest is basically broadways (card combinations of 10, J, Q, K, and A), especially of the same suit. KQ, AJ, AT, QJ, JT and other such hands can still have favorable implied odds as they dominate part of the villain's range, which tends to open hands like J-9, K-9, KT, QT, Q- 9 etc.

Post-flop, as the stacks will usually not be very large in relation to the size of the pot, we must aggressively draw, as this adds up the fairness of the hand when we force the villain to fold.

The advantage of having a strong flat call range is that we are unlikely to be bad on a flop. There will almost always be a chance to improve the hand: a backdoor flush or straight, or simply overcards, which favors simple and basic moves like the float and raise in continuation bet (exploiting the trend of more c-betting players). times than they should).

Top mistakes of beginning players

By far, and I don't have to think too hard to come to this conclusion, the most common mistake I see in beginning players with medium stacks is, again, to play very passively. You waste big chips making a lot of preflop calls and calling draws with the river. In addition, it is common to see players rushing with small pairs, opening or calling raises in bad situations.

Following this passive trend, not having a 3-bet light range today can be considered a failure as it makes your game very predictable and easy to exploit.

There is much more to talk about playing with medium stacks. The particularities of the tournaments and opponents we face force us to make very important adjustments. Depending on the level of the game, for example, there is no need for a 3-bet light range, as opponents do not seek to exploit this flaw and do not know how to react correctly.

Playing Deep Stack

Earlier, I talked about the game with short and medium stacks. Now , let's talk about the deep stacked game.

In general, players with more cash game experience have a greater knowledge of the subject than tournament players. This is obviously because they are more used to working the postflop game and to better size their bets.

Mainly because they spend most of their time playing stacks of up to 40 big blinds, most tournament players make conceptual mistakes, ranging from hand selection to betting size, and end up playing quite exploitably. However, mastering the fundamentals of deep play is very important, as this is the only stack track that players, due to the early game, will always play in tournaments. Big events tend to start with 200 to 300 bbs stack.

In tournaments, any table where the effective stack is over 50 bbs, the game can already be considered deep. This is the type of stack we will deal with below.

Ranges for the deep stack game

Contrary to short and medium stacks, there is a lot of postflop in deep play - and more importantly, room for postflop maneuvering because of the high SPR (see ed. 76) . That means we will constantly get to the river. That is, we must select hands that have the potential to improve in the future.

What does that mean? "Dominated" hands lose value, like ATo and KJo. Already suited hands, especially connectors, and AXs are better because they have nut potential.

Playing in position in a deep game is much more important. Playing low SPRs, the position loses a lot of value as the game often comes down to hitting and missing the board. However, with high SPRs, there are many paths to be traced to the river, where dropping your top pair and the like is frequent.

Therefore we should play really tighter from early position and looser from late position, especially against weaker players.

3-bet and 4-bet in the deep stack game

3-betting in deep does not need to be as polarized as in short. There will be a lot more postflop here, including 3-bet pots. It is common, for example, for regulars to 3-bet against weaker players with strong hands who are not comfortable facing a 4-bet. For that, they use "the best hands that would fold".

For example, 100-200 blinds, 20,000 stacks. Villain (weak player with poor postflop) opens 500 from UTG. Hero from UTG + 1 has KQs. We have good reason to 3-bet here: position over villain, decent hand in a situation where we showed a lot of strength. But the main reason for 3-betting is that we have isolated the game against a weak postflop player.

When it comes to 4-betting, then we need to be more polarized, especially in games up to 100 bbs, where if there is a postflop, the SPR will be low. If when we apply a deep stacked 3-bet, blockers, for example, lose a lot of value - since there is a lot of postflop play - in 4-bet situations they are important again because there is a greater tendency for the game to resolve. still preflop.

Size of bets

The default for bet sizes with stacks up to 30 bbs are generally small, close to the minimum allowable bet. This works well because there are usually not as many pots with more than two players, especially in the higher blinds, and weak hand ranges remain for postflop play. In the case of 3-bets, they usually vary between 2.2 and 2.5 times the previous bet, because with short and medium stacks there is almost no 3-bet call.

However, in a deep game, pre-flop mini-raises and 30% continuation bets (c-bets) from the pot can cause problems in the future, as there is a tendency to keep many players in the hand. Another problem is that it doesn't help define the ranges we face and let alone extract value as we hit the river with a small pot.

Playing out of position, increasing bet sizes, both preflop and post, helps to defend mainly against good players, as raises, c-betting and float are more expensive, which reduces their frequency. Speaking especially of out-of-position 3-bets, be careful not to make your opponent's life much easier by making very small bets compared to the stack they are playing.

Top mistakes of beginning players

Relying mainly on the early levels of the big tournaments, where everyone has big and similar stacks (and in the final straights there are other factors, such as prize pressure), the main mistakes less prepared players often make are wrong bet sizes, distorted ranges and excess limps.

The weaker players think a lot about "protecting" the hand they are playing with and forget about "playing the hand itself", ie extracting value when drawing and folding when necessary.

At the same time, I find more senior players pre-flop mini-raising with a table full of high-stakes calling stations. The result is: dozens of pots with many players, which reduces the success rate.

Regarding limps, there are virtually no situations where open limp will be a good move. When the player chooses to open the hand only by calling the blind, the result is that he will be completely dependent on the texture of the board and will face more than one player, drastically reducing the chance of winning the hand. But even worse, he will end up losing most of the pots to the bluff of some competent player who will exploit him.

Regarding ranges, it is common to see players losing big pots with weak hands, such as top pair or even middle pair. You need to think a little more about the ranges you are facing and visualize the scenarios for future streets. Concepts such as implied and reverse odds and SPR should be the main drivers of postflop play.

I hope this chapter helps you, the reader, to ground your moves by adapting to each new stack range during tournaments. And remember the basis of them all: play aggressively.

Fábio Eiji -
https://cardplayer.com.br/revistas/78/estrategias-
basicas-por-faixa-de-stack-parte-i/1896

8.5 Training and proposed exercises

Exercise 1

Scenario

Only eight players remain in contention for the title of a major 6-Max tournament. At a table with three other opponents, you have 345,000, one of the biggest stacks in the room. At the moment, the blinds are at 2,500 / 5,000 before 500.

Straight from small, a competitor with 305,000 raises to 13,000. With 2 ♠ 2 ♦ , you choose to defend the big and announce the call.

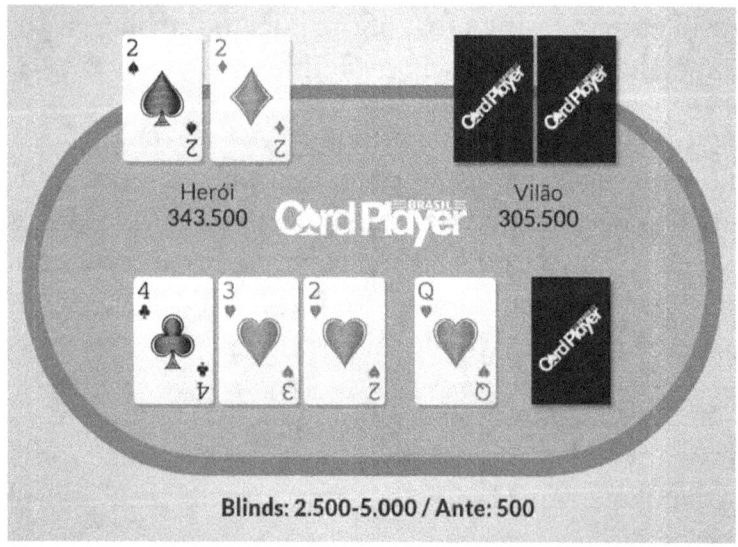

On the 4 ♣ 3 ♥ 2 ♥ flop , the villain c-bet 15,000, which causes you to raise to 50,000. With your opponent's call, the turn comes with a Q ♥ .

This time, your opponent just checks.

Questions

Do you pass the turn or bet? If you check, talk about your river strategy. If you choose to bet, how much will it be? Because of your opponent's willingness to call your flop raise, what types of hands are in your range?

Before seeing the author's analysis of the book and the outcome of the play, exercise, try to project the most lucrative move in the face of the situation.

_____

_____

_____

_____

_____

_____

_____

_____

_____

Author's Opinion:

Given the situation presented, I very rarely give a free card to the villain on TURN, because having a set I have to extract value from speculative hands, such as flush draw, draw of sequence (missing a card for sequence), which most of the time will not come in the RIVER.

But how much to bet, to bet?

I don't like values too high to scare the villain, nor do I see profitability in betting less than 30% of the pot in this situation, so I usually bet about 45% of the amount I already have in the pot.

The villain calling and RIVER beating the card possible, me playing in position, talking last, I check, I check if he makes this move and consider folding if he bets something. In general I do not invest more chips in RIVER, because the villain will hardly pay me losing, so I see in TURN the last opportunity to increase my win.

Outcome

On board 4 ♣ 3 ♥ 2 ♥ Q ♥ , after Jan Suchanek's check with 2 ♠ 2 ♦ , Jason Gray also passed the turn. The river revealed a 6 ♥ and Suchanek bet 100,000. Gray dropped his cards to see Suchanek pull the pot in the Asia Pacific WSOP Event 4 with K ♦ 5 ♥ .

Conclusion

The author of the book would have lost his hand, even playing differently, but, as already mentioned, the villain will hit his card in RIVER in a few opportunities, as one must think of long-term profitability, cannot be results oriented.

https://cardplayer.com.br/noticias/mao-da-semana-cardplayer-brasil/17618

Exercise 2

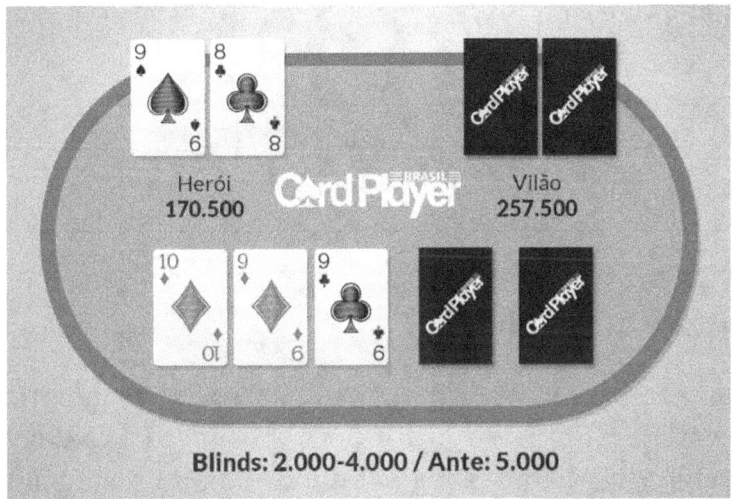

Scenario

A big tournament has 68 players in the title fight, but only 63 will get ITM. In the 2,000 / 4,000 blinds before 500 you have 170,500 chips, which leaves you with 42 bbs.

From the start of the table, a 257,500 competitor raises to 8,000. The action comes to you, who at 9 ♠ 8 ♣ 3-bet 23,000 straight from the small. Big drops his cards, while the aggressor increases to 41,000. You think a lot before you call.

On the 10 ♦ 9 ♦ 9 ♣ flop , in front of a check, the villain bets 29,500. You still have 129,000.

Questions

Do you call or raise? In case of a raise, say how much it will be. If you pay, talk about your strategy for the turn.

What do you do?

_____

_____

_____

_____

_____

Author's Opinion:

This exercise is appropriate to raise a very important question. The Hero (98) does not need would get involved in a hand, being out of position against a villain who opened the pot at the beginning of the table, remembering that being in the position SMALL BLIND is the first to speak in the FLOP , TURN and RIVER out of position with about 40 BB of chips such movement is unnecessary. If Villain had made the same bet in late position, in the middle of the table, or in BTN , a position before SMALL BLIND , one could imagine that he would be just stealing blinds and taking advantage of the pressure of the "bubble", with only the elimination of 5 players to enter the prize pool.

However, in the situation, Villain's hand range would really be between high pairs or strong aces, such as: JJ, QQ, KK, QQ, AQ, AK or even AJ. Therefore it would be unprofitable to face potential hands with 98 out of position on FLOP , TURN or RIVER .

Again, it is important to remember that you cannot study results-oriented, as in the example presented, FLOP presented T 99, a dream that happens in a very small% of times.

Outcome

Faced with a bet of 29,500 on the flop 10 ♦ 9 ♦ 9 ♣ , with 9 ♠ 8 ♣ , Binh Nguyen moved all-in. Corey Hochman called and showed A ♠ A ♥ . Turn J ♥ and river K ♥ kept Nguyen's lead and he doubled his chips at the LA Poker Classic.

Conclusion

In this exercise rather emphasize that dev to assess any movement before applying it , but it made a move not very good, as the exposed, happening unlikely, as FLOP T99, must make the most of the villain, as indeed over happening against the pair of defeated aces.

https://cardplayer.com.br/noticias/mao-da-semana-cardplayer-bras//18677

Exercise 3

Scenario

You're in the heads-up of one of the top super high rollers of the season. In the 30,000 / 60,000 blinds with 60,000 big blind, you have a stack of 3,765,000. The leader, a pro with a fantastic career in cash games and MTTs, owns 7,040,000.

When you get Q ♦ 2 ♠ , you raise to 150,000 straight from the button. The villain, in turn, applies the call. On the A ♠ 10 ♦ 8 ♦ flop , in front of a check, you bet 235,000. Your opponent chooses to pay.

Then the turn reveals a 3 ♦ . After a new check from villain, you push 515,000 and receive the call.

Finally, the river comes with a 6 ♥ . The villain checks.

What do you do?

_____

_____

_____

_____

_____

_____

_____

_____

_____

Try to put yourself in the above situation and choose to check and hand the pot as you have no pair with Q as the high card, or try to bluff to collect a nice pot of chips.

Author's Opinion:

In TURN, when villain called 515,000 Bet, it is hard to imagine that he had no pair at hand , in RIVER the bluff would have to be very loud or ALL IN, so in this case it is advisable to check or fold in RIVER for any bet.

Outcome

On board A ♠ 10 ♦ 8 ♦ 3 ♦ 6 ♥ , with Q ♦ 2 ♠ , Alex Foxen answered his compatriot Isaac Haxton's check with a bet of 1,400,000. At the head of qualifying, Haxton announced all-in. Foxen dropped his cards and saw his opponent show K ♦ 6 ♦ .

https://cardplayer.com.br/noticias/mao-da-semana-cardplayer-brasil/19434

Exercise 4

Scena

rio

Five players remain in the fray for the title of a super high roller. In the 20,000 / 40,000 blinds with 40,000 big blind, you have a comfortable stack of 2,205,000 chips.

In UTG, you get 4 ♠ 4 ♥ and raise to 90,000. The action reaches even small, a businessman with several impressive results in live and online MTTs. Owner of 1,420,000, he chooses to pay.

After the opening of 8 ♥ 7 ♣ 4 abertura , in front of a check, you bet 90,000 . The villain responds with a raise to 335,000. You pay. In turn 9 ♣ , your opponent pushes 275,000 to the center of the table. You call again. Finally, on the river K ♦ , the villain announces 720,000 all-in.

Answer if you would call with your set of 4 on RIVER, the villain's all-in 720,000 . You have a stack of 1,525,000 in , losing that would leave you with 805,000, 20bb.

_____
_____
_____
_____
_____ ___

Author's Opinion:

In particular, it would be very difficult for me to fold my set of 4 at RIVER because I still have 805,000 chips left, and for my playing style, the remaining 20 big blinds in chips would still be able to continue my course in the tournament. . But I warn the villain raising on the FLOP, because it indicates a lot of strength, but it is difficult for us to see ghosts, with a bigger set on the flop than ours. If you chose to fold in RIVER, rest assured, it would not be a bad move either, as you have 3 suited cards with a flush chance on the board 8 7 9.

Outcome

On board 8 ♥ 7 ♣ 4 ♣ 9 ♣ K ♦ , Briton Talal Shakerchi put his whole stack into play. Holding 4 ♠ 4 ♥ , Adrián Mateos opted to call and saw his opponent show 7 ♠ 7 ♦ . Shakerchi pulled the pot and went for $ 300. Super High Roller Bowl.

Conclusion

I want to conclude this exercise by mentioning that there are no unique decisions to make in certain situations, it is important to know how to evaluate the risks of the results. As I mentioned in the exercise above, I would call RIVER for leaving me 20 BB if I lost, but there are players who don't feel confident continuing a tournament with that many blinds, so if you only feel comfortable playing over 30 bb, for example, evaluate the risks more carefully before making the decision.

https://cardplayer.com.br/noticias/mao-da-semana-cardplayer-brasil/19408

Exercise 5

Scenario

You are playing the most expensive tournament in poker history. The field is made up exclusively of amateur players . Although you are not a pro, you are more experienced than most of your opponents.

Seven entrants are still in the title race, with only six going to receive at least € 1.5 million. In total, the champion will take home € 11,111,111.

With 21,050,000 chips, you occupy the third position. The blinds are at 250,000 / 500,000 with before 75,000. Among his opponents, only one is short with 16 bbs.

The table folds to you, who from small, with J ♣ 7 ♠ , chooses to raise to 1,400,000. Big, who is second with 27.7 million, pays.

After the 6 ♠ 5 ♦ 4 ♥ flop , you pass the turn. The villain bets 1,000,000 and hears the call. On turn J ♠ , you make a new check. The villain pushes 3,000,000 to the center of the table. The pot is 8,325,000 and its stack is 18,575,000.

Questions

Do you fold, call or raise? If you announce the raise, talk about how much it will be. Are you going to raise for value or bluff? In case of a call, talk about your river strategy?

_____
_____
_____
_____
_____
_____
_____
_____
_____
_____
_____

Author's Opinion:

In this situation, I need to remind you about the concept of ICM when we are competing for the awards in the finals. Being among the 3 players in chips, it is not profitable in the long run to make moves where the risk is to be eliminated before a player who has fewer chips than you. You can play pots that don't expose your entire chip stack, so evaluate the situation and consider playing more tightly only in these situations. But beware, in a few moves the table composition can change completely, so you have to play more aggressively, even if you have to risk all your chips. In the situation in question I would also only check and call bet of value that did not compromise me, even hitting top pair in TURN, because the board was well connected.

Outcome

Faced with a 3,000,000 bet on the board 6 ♠ 5 ♦ 4 ♥ J ♠ , with J ♣ 7 ♠ , James Bord announced the call. On river 8 ♦ , Bord passed the turn. Russian Anatoly Gurtovoy did the same and showed 4 ♣ 4 ♦ , cards that did not yield him the pot in the Big One For One Drop Extravaganza.

https://cardplayer.com.br/noticias/mao-da-semana-cardplayer-bras//16371

CHAPTER 9

EFFECTS OF EMOTIONAL AND BEHAVIOR FACTORS ON POKER

Most poker players have heard that poker is a people game, not a card game, so the emotional factors will be key to achieving poker success, and these factors must be addressed not only from opponents, but also from opponents. also from the player himself. In other words, it is not enough to identify your opponents if the player itself does not know how they are viewed by them. This self-criticism is the hardest to do, but anyone who dominates this situation will always be ahead of their opponents, thinking outside the box.

Before we can worry about poker math, we need to pay attention to the most important factor of the game: the players themselves. After all, poker is a game of people, each with their own way of playing and their style of play.

But how to identify the style of opponents? What profiles can they adopt? Here, we'll look at how to spot opponent trends, and then define strategies to counter each type. If you do it correctly, you are likely to come out as the big winner of the night.

As we said in the previous article, we assume that you already know the basic rules of Texas Hold'em. If you have never played before, take a look at this interactive tutorial before reading on.

TYPES

The Loose-aggressive Maniac

It is the most common player in poker nights. He is always after action and loves to bet, bluff and play many - or even all - hands. He always has a pretext for getting in hand.

This guy looks for adrenaline more than victory, although sometimes he wins out on a lucky night. Above all, a loose-aggressive player is looking for a good time, and doesn't have much to do with the chips, perhaps because he has taken a few extra bucks during the game.

Tactics

Beware of maniacs: it's hard to bluff against them, and your stack is at risk all the time. The best thing to do is to play strong hands and incomplete hands, also known as "speculative draws" (for example, four cards of the same suit, one missing for the flush), and wait for the maniac to try to bluff when you have a strong game. This is how you will take his chips.

The Loose-Passive

This is a very curious type, as it usually plays the opposite of what is theoretically considered correct. He comes in with weak hands and pays all the time hoping to hit very difficult hands.

Ironically, this player calls instead of betting when he has a strong hand, and does not raise, failing to extract chips with hands that really have value.

And don't moan when you find a calling station holding the best possible hand that round. Instead, be pleased that you lost a lot less chips than you would if you were facing a strong opponent.

Tactics

It is the easiest opponent to face. All you have to do is raise your hand to the end, because when it comes to showing the cards he will almost always have hands that will make you wonder "how did he call you?"

As with maniacs, don't try to bluff the payer. They simply do not understand what your bet means, and will frustrate you in their attempt.

The Rock (tight-passive)

You know that guy who spends all night without participating in the game, selecting the cards, and when he decides to bet ends up delivering that has a strong game, scaring everyone out of the hand? Well, that's the tight-passive player, rock hard.

Tactics

This guy is usually fearful, and against him the bluff becomes a great weapon. This guy is terrified of losing chips and always sees on the table a monster that will defeat his game.

Unless you have a very strong combination, he will probably fold if you bet. If he is suddenly ecstatic, run away, for he certainly has a very strong game.

The Shark (tight-aggressive)

It is the player you must be. You don't play a lot of hands, but when you get into the game you win.

Since you don't play every hand like the maniac does, your opponents won't know when you have a strong hand, an incomplete hand, or just bluffing.

By selecting good hands, the chances of making a strong flop game are greater. Thus, the chances of you having the best hand also increase. This greatly facilitates your game and your victory.

Tactics

If you find another shark on the table, avoid facing it unless you have a very strong hand right now.

Remember there are plenty of ducks for both of you to hunt and do well on poker night.

Take note

Loose - plays a lot of hands

Tight - select more hands to play

Aggressive - bet a lot

Passive - give up easily, and pay more than you bet

https://cardplayer.com.br/especiais/patonuncamais/cara-a-cara/20

9.1 Identifying Players in the Online Game with HUD Information

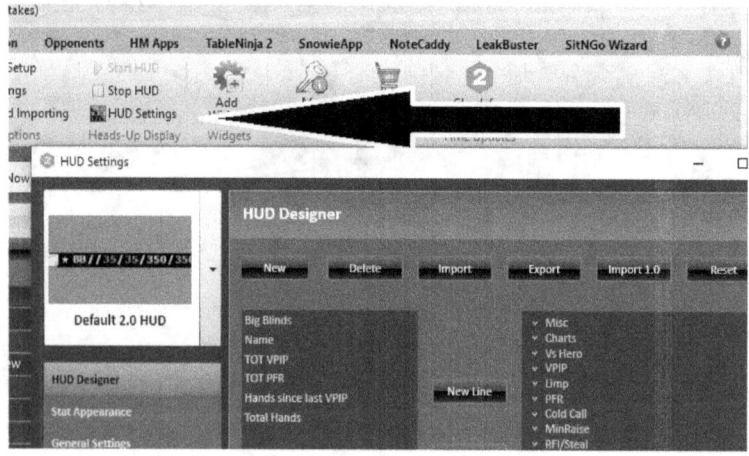

Virtually all supporting software in this category offers a setup option. I recommend setting it up very simply with the most important statistics, such as: VPiP (% of times the player enters the pot), PFR, PFR (% of times the player raises before the flop, "Preflop raise"), Big Blinds (amount of big blind the player currently has), Player Name, Hands Since VPip wool (how many hands the player is not participating) and Total Hands (amount of hands stored, remembering, the larger the sample, the more faithful will be the portrait of the statistic).

I present above my statistics in a poker tournament with 67 hands played, I played 17% (VPiP), increasing 18% (RPF) a very solid profile.

With these statistics it is possible to profile the player in online poker, alias is one of the questions many people ask, how to read players in online poker.

For example, players who enter the pot by more than 40% are considered loose players, and if they have low PFR (less than half of VPiP), they are loose-passive players. "Flopinho", example: VPiP 44%, PFR 7%. To project possible hands (range or range of hands) that player, you can use free software like "Equilab" found for download on the site : pokerstrategy.com .

Important Information: Use this software for study purposes, with closed poker applications on Pokerstars, for example, when running it with Equilab open, you will receive a message that is in violation of site policy:

" Hello,

We have noticed that you recently used a poker calculator tool (namely 'PokerStrategy Equilab') during the operation of the software. Certain features of this tool make it in violation of ours. "

Let's look at the example below, which would be the range of hands of this player, when he would enter the pot 44% and when he would raise by 7%. Note that the 7% turns out to be a player who raises with a narrow range of hands, meaning it would not be too difficult to know when he would have a good game before the flop.

Put% 44 on a player. ..

To see what the PFR would look like, just do the same later with 7 % - Clicking on the icons opens more options, the first icon is a graph, better to understand.

Note that 44% represents almost half of the deck, so you can imagine a very large amount of combination. Don't worry, over time, when you hit that same 44% or 41%, you'll already know more or less which range you're facing.

AA	AKs	AQs	AJs	ATs	A9s	A8s	A7s	A6s	A5s	A4s	A3s	A2s
AKo	KK	KQs	KJs	KTs	K9s	K8s	K7s	K6s	K5s	K4s	K3s	K2s
AQo	KQo	QQ	QJs	QTs	Q9s	Q8s	Q7s	Q6s	Q5s	Q4s	Q3s	Q2s
AJo	KJo	QJo	JJ	JTs	J9s	J8s	J7s	J6s	J5s	J4s	J3s	J2s
ATo	KTo	QTo	JTo	TT	T9s	T8s	T7s	T6s	T5s	T4s	T3s	T2s
A9o	K9o	Q9o	J9o	T9o	99	98s	97s	96s	95s	94s	93s	92s
A8o	K8o	Q8o	J8o	T8o	98o	88	87s	86s	85s	84s	83s	82s
A7o	K7o	Q7o	J7o	T7o	97o	87o	77	76s	75s	74s	73s	72s
A6o	K6o	Q6o	J6o	T6o	96o	86o	76o	66	65s	64s	63s	62s
A5o	K5o	Q5o	J5o	T5o	95o	85o	75o	65o	55	54s	53s	52s
A4o	K4o	Q4o	J4o	T4o	94o	84o	74o	64o	54o	44	43s	42s
A3o	K3o	Q3o	J3o	T3o	93o	83o	73o	63o	53o	43o	33	32s
A2o	K2o	Q2o	J2o	T2o	92o	82o	72o	62o	52o	42o	32o	22

Now let's see what range of hands this player would be raising before the flop (RPF) with 7% of the cards.

Below is a compact table of possible hand ranges based on% VPiP. It is interesting to use it in the learning phase.

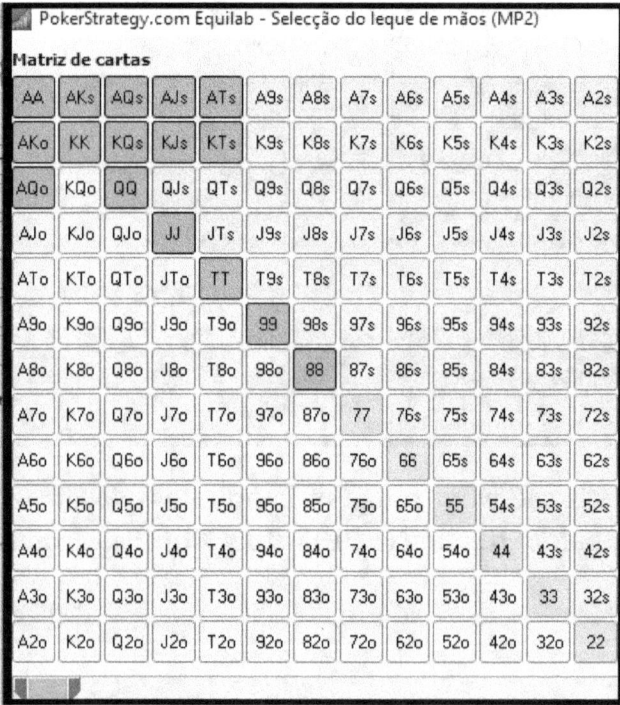

One tip I always give in my videos is so that players are not always conditioned to these tables, which is used only as a parameter, because a very important detail is that the% VPiP will depend on the table the player is playing, As a rule, one should always play the opposite of the flow, ie if the table is playing several players with very high VPip, it is profitable that we play tighter, harder or very close to "rock". Or, if you have more locked players at the table playing too few hands, it is best to play more hands by pressing the table to collect chips.

One more important factor is to notice our statistics as well, because most of the time, other players will be evaluating us at the tables. Then make analysis of the opponents statistics and your own.

9.2 Placing Hand Ranges by Profile

At the beginning, in the learning phase, it is recommended to play with a narrow range of hands, between 5% and 15%, but it is good to try to evolve the line of reasoning that good cards do not always guarantee the end result, but The player's attitude can yield many pots. In other words, we don't have to wait until "AA" comes, we can play any two cards as if we had this pair in hand.

Perfil	FREQUÊNCIA	RANGE OU GAMA
a Rocha (tight-passive)	5%	88+, ATs+, KQs, AKo
	10%	77+, A9s+, KTs+, QTs+, AJo+
	15%	77+, A7s+, K9s+, QTs+ JTs, ATo+, KTo+, QJo
o Shark (tight-aggressive)	20%	66+, A4s+, K7s+, Q9s+ J9s+, T9s, A9o+, KTo+ QTo+, JTo
	25%	66+, A2s+, K6s+, Q8s+ J8s+, T8s+, A7o+, K9o+ QTo+, JTo
	35%	55+, A2s+, K3s+, Q5s+ JTs+, T7s+, 97s+, 87s A4o+, K8o+, Q9o+, J9o+ T9o
o Maniaco (loose-aggressive)	50%	33+, A2s+, K2s+, Q2s+ J4s+, T6s+, 96s+, 86s+ 76s, 65s, A2o+, K5o+ Q7o+, J7o+, T7o+, 98o
	75%	22+, A2s+, K2s+, Q2s+ J2s+, T2s+, 92s+, 83s+ 73s+, 63s+, 52s+, 43s, A2o+, K2o+, Q2o+, J4o+ T6o+, 96o+, 86o+, 75o+, 65o

Remembering that the game of poker is a game of representation and not of cards.

Note that the player profile "Shark" is linked to the balanced range, not too rock nor too loose. This is not to say that sometimes the SHARK player does not go out of standard, such as playing rock in the early stages of a tournament, or looser at a shy table where players are locked. So be aware and consider how many hands were observed from the players, as has been said, the larger the sample, the more accurate the information will be.

9. 3 Notes x HUD

Using assistive software does not guarantee maximization of profitability, because many users have a hard time analyzing the data, or set up to display many statistics, which causes pollution on the computer screen. Some third party software is prohibited on some websites, so it is good that we players are not dependent on these applications.

There is also a current evolving on online platforms, including those that today accept the use of applications, in the sense of prohibition, in order to honor fair play among its players.

Also, I know a lot of professional gamers who have never used such apps and are profitable, so if you can't make it profitable and put your HUD to use or not, you're completely wrong.

Some precautions should be taken for non-HUDs, taking notes from players, all online poker platforms offer this feature, including the option to color avatars and play carefully at non-HUD tables.

Remember that in the live game there is no HUD! But you can use the same Profile / Frequency / Range table to help with decisions.

9.4 - The trust factor

Alan Schoonmaker: "How could I be such an idiot?" Is the title of my first article in this series [Card Player Brasil, Issue 117] that I've been writing and the first question in Jason Zweig's fascinating book, Your Money & Your Brain. Money & Your Brain). It was written for investors - and poker is a form of investment. This book proves that our brains make us think we are much smarter than we really are.

Taking advantage of the above, I would like to point out Alan Schoonmaker's book , **"YOUR BIGGEST POKER ENEMY",** was the second book I read, just as I started playing poker in mid-2009. I knew the biggest enemy is ourselves, the players themselves, but reading is paramount to thinking of a poker mindset, when you learn to do your self-criticism and if you finish the book, you'll be able to handle the pressure in poker. .

In return, the trust factor is essential in everything in life, at work, in study, in relationship, in sport, in driving a vehicle. So when playing poker, if you don't have confidence, take a break!

To insist on poker without being sure of your goals is to throw money in the trash. It takes confidence even to have fun at the tables.

Lack of confidence creates uncertainty, and undecided people cannot be good investors or poker players. Just a very important detail, trust does not come from luck, it comes from knowledge, the more knowledge one has gained on a subject, the greater the confidence to practice. I can sum it up in one sentence: "The more I study, the luckier I am!".

On the other hand, overconfidence is everywhere, and since everything in excess is harmful to health, it would be no different in poker. I have seen situations where a player in a poker tournament, pulling a lot of chips in his arm, when all of a sudden overconfidence in everything was working out, makes a high-risk move and ends up being knocked out of the tournament when that player blames her. Bad luck in this situation is because it is contaminated with overconfidence.

9.5 - Assessing Risks

Humans don't like 50:50 bets. If I offered you an equal money bet on a round of coins for $ 1000, the vast majority of you would say no. If you had no choice in the matter and were forced to bet, you would probably react with discomfort and fear - praying not to lose would be a more common reaction than getting excited about the chance to win. This risk prevention process is a survival mechanism that has been responsible for the success of our species. In poker, however, it is a huge obstacle in the path of progress.

The failure in risk assessment in poker is caused by the belief that to make an investment, the situation must be more favorable than 50:50.

As we will see, this is almost never the case.

What is a 50:50 bet on Poker?

When it comes to facing a bet or raise, there is basically no 50:50 decision. If the pot was completely empty and I bet $ X, you would need 50% equity to make the call and draw. This is because you are investing a unit to win a unit, or in terms of poker, your pot odds are 1: 1. This situation almost never exists due to the gradual growth of the pot. There is almost always some dead money that we can add to the payout payout: investment rate. Even if the pot is only $ 10 and you bet on a huge overbet of $ 50, I'll have a pot odds of 60:50 or 1.2: 1. That means I need 45% equity to make up for my payout, Call.

Even when facing a huge overbet, we still need to be good less than half the time to pay.

A true 50:50 can only be a bet on a completely empty pot, and so, for all instructional purposes, we can say that a 50:50 when a bet does not exist in poker.

The process of subconscious risk assessment, the subconscious mind is programmed with a very definite test to find out whether or not to take a risk. In a healthy human adult, it looks something like:

Take the risk only if the average result is significantly good rather than bad.

This leads us to instinctively reject 50:50 investments and even turn down some opportunities that are a little better than bad. I would be willing to bet that most of you reading this would also turn down my coin tossing proposal, even if I paid you and extra $ 20 in addition to the $ 1000 profit you made. You are inclined to reject this clearly lucrative bet because of the "significant" part of the above risk assessment test that runs automatically in your subconscious mind. This test is there to protect you from withstanding high levels of stress and volatility for minimal gains, this would hurt your chances of survival. Unfortunately, to be successful in poker, resisting high levels of stress and minimal gain volatility is something we have to do over and over again. It is now becoming clear that the subconscious mind and its risk assessment program fail in the realm of poker and undermine our chances of success. If you held JJ preflop and knew I had all-in (in an almost empty pot) with AKo, you should call, like it or not. You have 55% equity and need 50% (or a little less when you remember that the blinds are acting like dead money).

Poker Risk Assessment Failures

The most common bet size we are likely to find on the river is about 75% of the pot. When we face a $ 7.50 bet on a $ 10 pot, we are getting 17.5: 7.5 or 2.33: 1. That means our mandatory stake is only 30%. Unfortunately, the conscious mind is so busy calculating the villain's range that it forgets to remember this very low target value. The subconscious mind takes on this task and chants its deceptive mantra: "the result must be significantly better than bad." In numerical terms, the subconscious is demanding that we have something like 55% equity to call - how absurd!

In fact, the 2.33: 1 pot odds mean that the result can be significantly worse than good and the call can still be profitable in the long run. If Villain is bluffing just a third of the time, you can make a profitable call with your bluff catcher. Many aspiring players give up here, not because they misunderstand their opponent's range, but because they subconsciously set a ridiculously hard target for themselves when it comes to being good more than half the time. This is crazy when we understand the odds of the pot correctly.

The Solution- The true equity needed to place a bet is counterintuitive to the subconscious mind. It will always tend to grossly overestimate how often we need to earn before we make an investment. The best way to learn a better poker risk assessment test is to assign this task to the conscious mind, at least until it becomes second nature. When you face a bet on the river, or an all-in before the river, the spot is simple enough that the required equity and real capital is all that matters. There are no implied chances or future fold equity to distort the image. At these points, start by stating your pot odds and resulting in the required equity. Only then should you start analyzing the villain's range and how often you think you can win by calling. Do this consciously at first until it becomes second nature. This may take weeks or months, but it will be worth it in the long run. The brain must learn that the normal risk assessment test that serves us so well in life does not apply to poker. We should stop making bad bends due to an absurd risk assessment test!

Pete Clarke article, Pokerstars.com blog

9.6 Dealing with Downswing

Find out why downswings happen in poker and how you can handle them so you can keep playing with confidence.

Knowing that happiness is a choice does not mean that every time you are sad or angry, you can be suddenly happy. "Explicit" knowledge is not enough to drag you out of your cave. For this change of emotions to happen, you have to experience this transformation so often that it becomes an automated response.

When this happens, through experience, practice, and wisdom - you will have developed "tacit" knowledge, and it brings me back to the " Calmning Strategies" poster that adorns the closet under my girlfriend.

The 11 Calming Strategies - Most of you reading this will have 'Explicit' knowledge of how to calm down when feeling angry, sad and even intensified feelings of happiness. Achieving emotional balance is vital when going downswing.

Using these strategies becomes self-contained, or you create such a keen sense of attention that the results in the tables do not produce the emotional storms that can turn a 43-year-old professional poker player into a two-year-old.

Before you deploy the 11 calming strategies, you need a reminder to use them at the right time. Do not leave gold inside the wallet.

BJ Fogg is a behavioral scientist at Stanford University and a specialist in developing habits change through a philosophy known as Tiny Little Habits.

Here's Fogg during a TEDx speech at Tiny Little Habits.

Fogg calls his behavioral model B + MAP.

Behavior = Motivation, Ability and Prompt.

In this case, your motivation for change is your desire to be a better poker player. Your ability to change depends on turning the 11 Soothing Strategies into "Tacit" knowledge, leading to a mindfulness mindset that reduces the adverse effect a downswing has on your life. The warning is the card I used to have in my wallet. I suggest you get yours out of your wallet.

A prompt is not a prompt if you cannot see it.

You do not need to use a card as a prompt. Most importantly, use a consistent activity as a prompt. You may be able to use the prompt to enter your wallet as a signal to read a note or listen to an audio recording you have made by remembering to use a calming strategy.

Maybe you can use the toilet warning. Think about your game, the ever-changing environments, and choose a habit that you can turn into an anchor that leads you to a calming strategy. (A classic anchor habit is brushing my teeth - after cleaning my teeth, I will run).

Next, it's crucial as you begin to feel an emotion that can lead to leaning on or off the tables you first check with yourself and ask - what feeling is present right now?

You'll be surprised how many people can't express their feelings, so to help you out, here is a list of emotions:

Writing down your emotions helps reduce anxiety and stress, as mindfulness becomes the catalyst for change.

Once you understand how you are feeling, it's time to look at the children's poster and select the 11 calming strategies.

1. Close your eyes

Closing your eyes allows you to turn off external stimuli, allowing your body and mind to return to a state of homeostasis. You can do this right away while at the table, or you can leave the table to find a quiet place to do it.

2. Have a drink

Dehydration leads to anxiety, and there are also studies showing that drinking water strengthens your muscles and that water has soothing natural properties. Do not drink alcohol as a way to calm down, because alcohol creates more anxiety and dehydrates you.

3. Stretch your body

Stretching increases blood flow, thus relaxing the tension in the muscles. It is also the perfect way to induce mindfulness and find a more focused attitude. You must often stretch while playing poker.

4. Embrace a stuffed animal or a human.

Embracing increases our oxytocin levels, leading to an amplified wellness factor as it decreases cortisol, the stress hormone. It is also a fantastic and immediate mood change because we are conditioned to feel good or safe during a hug.

5. Take 3 Deep Breaths

As you slow your breathing and become more alert, your heart rate decreases, reducing stress and anxiety. Another great way to incorporate breathing into your soothing strategies around the poker table is to have a meditation app on your phone like Sam Harris's "Waking Up" that has a series of 10 minute meditations you can listen to before you play. again.

6. Draw-on Paper

One way to remove stress and anxiety from your body is to transfer these thoughts and feelings to paper. Focusing on drawing, or coloring, pushes your mind away from the pressure of the game and allows you to enter a mini-state of flow, enhancing your creativity.

7. Read a book

Like Jonathan Haidt's "Happiness Hypothesis"!

8. Think of a happy thought.

An excellent way to evoke happy thinking is to create a playlist that immediately evokes a sense of nostalgia. Gratitude is also crucial here. You can pair this with "drawing" above. Quickly draw or write down a list of things you're grateful for and this will put your downswing in perspective.

9. Make a puzzle

Similar to the drawing.

Focusing on something else allows you to go into a mini-flow state and take you away from the ugly side of the game.

10. Count to ten

See breathing and closing your eyes.

11. Squeeze a Ball

When you are anxious and stressed, your body tightens your muscles. Having something practical to tighten helps remind the brain to release this tension. Just make sure you don't choose to squeeze the neck of the person who just took you down to rate the city.

Yes, that's it.

You don't have to go to an online poker training site or hire a life coach. We all know that these strategies work, but we don't use them often enough to turn explicit knowledge into tacit understanding that fills the minds of the best players in the world.

Nail it and it's child's play.

Lee Davy article - is a poker writer and live reporter who has worked for all the top names in the industry, including the WPT, the WSOP and 888poker.

9.7 Pros and Cons of Becoming a Professional Gamer

What sets poker apart from other hobbies is its latent potential to become more than just a hobby if you can become good enough. For some, becoming a professional is a dream that never happens, for others it is an accident that puts them to life. If you aspire to a career as a poker player one day, it is wise to understand the practicalities first. There are advantages and disadvantages to making this transition. As someone who has been a professional player and instructor for the past five years, I would like to give you my opinion on this important lifelong decision.

Pro: Doing what you love

As a teenager and young adult, I worked on some really demoralizing minimum wage jobs. The feeling of having to get out of bed to do something that was totally meaningless and unsatisfying really hurt. The idea of stacking shelves for eight hours caused me something that mixed dread with futility. I chased poker as obsessively as I could because I had this burning desire not to end up doing something that left me asking, 'Is that so?' Sure, there are many other careers besides poker, but if you're a naturally talented player with high work ethic, passion for the game, and high mental toughness, a poker career is one way to avoid the trap of simply surviving. work to enjoy the weekend. For me, it was the answer to an absolute lack of guidance in my professional life. I played games all my life. They have always been my escape and my passion. Making a career out of a game is like being told to be a child forever. Until that happens, you'll get a punch in the face for the bad variation for the first time... Let's talk about it.

Against: Variance, stress and insecurity

If the futile jobs I worked in in my early twenties had something for them, I was sure that I would receive my meager salary at the end of the month. In the first year I became a professional, I didn't have much coaching or book sales yet, so I relied completely on the tides of variation that didn't tear me at the tables. The reason I say 'trusted' is that I really didn't have the mental gaming experience to handle a massive crash during that first year. Working hard at your game and putting in 40 hours a week on the tables to break even for two months due to an unpleasant downswing can cause all kinds of anxiety and pressure you have never felt before. Doubts about your ability to do this suddenly become huge demons. Poker turns into your worst nightmare and will work to become twelve more unbearable times. But here is the good news: If you are a winning player, the next climb is just around the corner. The problem is that you have to avoid falling apart while waiting for it. Variation leads to stress - this is inevitable in a healthy human being, especially when it threatens his ability to pay the bills. Don't neglect your mind game if you decide to go the professional way - you'll need it. especially when it threatens your ability to pay the bills. Don't neglect your mind game if you decide to go the professional way -

you'll need it. especially when it threatens your ability to pay the bills. Don't neglect your mind game if you decide to go the professional way - you'll need it.

Pro: Freedom

Being able to take time off is amazing. Not having anyone breathing around your neck while you work is liberating. Being the one who sets your own deadlines brings with it a satisfying sense of control. Feeling productive and focused? Play overtime. Feeling slow? Go for a nap and come back later. This control over when you work is a real luxury and is without a doubt my favorite part of having a poker career. Poker gives you the option of traveling for live play or going to the field for a week to work on your game for eight hours a day without a single distraction. Even if the game becomes a bit repetitive at times, and the honeymoon period ends when you make poker a full time job, freedom is permanent. Beware, though, too much freedom is a bad thing for those of us who lack the willpower.

Against: Fierce Competition and Instability

The game moves so quickly at the professional level that if you neglect to study for a single month, you may be left behind and lose some of your winning rate. Information is everywhere today, so it's no wonder that even unnaturally gifted players can play a minimally lucrative game. This makes the professional's margin much smaller than it was in glory days, when all we needed was a brain and a computer to make money. In such a competitive arena lies the problem of long-term uncertainty. Can I still win the games in three years? What if online poker is banned by my government or so heavily taxed that I can't profit? Unless you make a lot of money and are at the top of the game, there will be some long-term uncertainty about going pro.

Pete Clarke @ Carroters article

https://www.pokerstarsschool.com/article/Pros-and-Cons-of-Turning-Professional-at-Poker

9.8 Main causes of poker player failure

When it comes to poker, a first important point to note is that "talent" is highly relative. Poker is a multidisciplinary game and has different dimensions, such as logical-mathematical, strategic, as well as psychological (in various aspects, such as concentration, organization and empathy), emotional, among others. This shows us that having ease in one area can help, but it is not enough. It is possible, for example, to be victorious even knowing little or nothing about mathematical concepts, but making up for this shortcoming with an enormous capacity for observing and adjusting to opponents, a feature that comes mainly from the experience accumulated in felts and perhaps in life outside them.

At the same time, mastering all mathematical and strategic concepts does not guarantee career success for a player who has difficulty controlling his emotional, psychological and financial status. A player who constantly lives with tilts, who disproportionately affects each bad beat, each defeat and who does not properly manage his losses is doomed to failure.

In order to help the early career reader, I will share some of the reasons, which I think are the main reasons, that influence the failure of a potential poker player.

Image: CardPlayer Magazine Brazil

KEEP CONFIDENT IN THE DETAILS

The more we study the game, the more we understand its mechanics. Poker is not just about good hands versus bad hands. Understanding this is a fundamental step in not being shaken by defeats, whose frequency is undoubtedly much higher than that of victories. Winning poker is different from winning a tournament, so we are not talking about catching less, but about our ability to absorb losses, analyze them, learn from them and be emotionally prepared for the next challenge.

KEEP HUMBLE IN VICTORIES

It is difficult to understand the true manifestations of the so-called variance in poker. We soon learned that long periods of loss are part of the daily life of any professional gambler, the famous downswings. But many people underestimate the other side of variance, the upswings. It's more or less that story: when I lose, it's unlucky; when I win, it is by competence. Neither this nor that. Especially when we talk about tournaments, it is possible to win even without proper preparation. That is why early wins can be very damaging to the career of a player who is not psychologically mature enough to understand the limits of his abilities. Any player who wins a tournament has certainly had his merits and has the great qualities needed for a poker player; However, as we said in the introduction, some qualities are no guarantee of long-term success.

PLAN YOUR FINANCIAL LIFE

This is the most delicate part in a poker player's life, in fact, in anyone's life. I have the impression that we Brazilians are not properly educated to take care of our financial lives.

Poker is a game that involves large amounts of money. Whether for an average student who starts working as a dealer and earns much more than the average job at his age and qualification, or for (mainly) young players who are starting to win their first table wins. If it is online then. After all, the prizes are in dollars.

In addition to my own experience, I have many close examples of players who have won a lot, but today they have very little or nothing. It is very difficult to contain the euphoria while playing well and things work out, but you must never lose sight of the fact that going through a period without wins is common and will probably happen to everyone.

Ideally, the player who is investing in his career has kept a "mattress" worth 1 to 2 years of his monthly spending, so that if things don't work out in the beginning, the pressure to pay the money will pay off. accounts do not directly interfere with your playing.

BEST PROFILE

What is in common between the three items mentioned above? In none of them were the skills at the table preponderant, but the ability to manage money, earnings and emotional control were the most prominent factors.

As stated in the introduction, there are many qualities that are part of the characteristics of a good poker player. I feel confident in stating, however, that the player who has the greatest chance of success has as main characteristics the ability to concentrate and observe and a certain psychological and emotional maturity. These features help maintain a certain coolness about the poker game by preventing emotional ties from being created with the tournament or cash game session in question, thus enabling better decisions to be made and avoiding further frustrations when Things don't work out. Not everything is relative, but poker is.

Fábio Fiji https://cardplayer.com.br/revistas/87/motivos-motivos-which-influencia-no-fracasso-de-poker-em-potencial/2059

9.9 Identifying and managing the comfort zone in poker

Play humans tend to make disastrous decisions under pressure, even in the legal sciences, when a person commits a crime under serious threat or acts in self-defense for being assaulted or raped.

In the subjective realm of poker, we know that everyone has some fears that can hinder decision making, so it is important to identify those fears in order to manage them.

The comfort zone in poker is a very important emotional factor to be identified as a player outside his comfort zone tends to make poor gambling decisions. In a broad sense, we have bankroll management, as we know that some players tend to play more "stuck" when their bankroll is about to end and this influences decision making. In this case, I recommend that you follow the bankroll management instructions on time.

It also identifies decisions hampered by the player's stack size during a game, it is common to see players with 18 or 20 big blinds playing push or fold (all or nothing). In practice if a player knows that they will have trouble playing at about 20bb or less, they should carefully evaluate situations in which the outcome may put them in that situation. Example: The player is about 30bb and makes the decision to try to bluff or steal blinds in a round due to table actions, but failure to play will result in the loss of 12bb, in which case a player will have difficulty conduct the games later, I recommend that the evaluation to execute the plan be rigorous.

When it comes to the stack comfort zone, I recommend training in shortstack games like SPIN AND GO. This is because in late tournament stages, it is rare to have a chance to play depstack with big stacks of chips. Maybe that's why there were a lot of phrases like, "I can easily get to the finals, but I can't win tournaments."

Another reason for worrying about the comfort zone is that experienced and professional players (sharks) identify this factor in their opponents, so if the villain is a shark, for example, it is very likely that he has already identified if you are in. or outside your comfort zone, and will easily be able to extract your chips with that information. This is one reason why players are winners or losers at tournament final tables.

Therefore, it is one more situation to apply Emotional Intelligence, identifying your comfort zone to be able to make the best decisions against players who will probably already have this information.

CHAPTER 10

TIPS FOR MANAGING VARIANCE

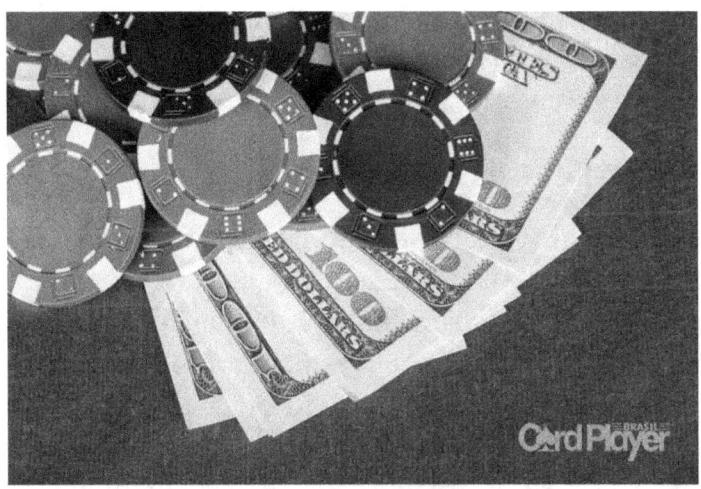

The variance is rough. The reason the short-term element of luck in poker worries us so much is that in real life we are not used to this volatility. Trying to adapt to the idea of doing the right things a few days and being punished mercilessly takes time and practice. Here are some tips to help you navigate the storm of variation and emerge from the other side with your mind game intact.

1. Play Minor Sessions

Students who play for four hours without rest end up tired and tired very quickly. The human ability to handle large amounts of luck is finite. Facing the twists and turns, positive or negative, generates high levels of emotion and consumes willpower. After an hour or two of playing poker, the human mind's ability to cope with variation diminishes as it tires, consuming energy in the form of self-control. Do not ease bending during sessions by extending the session beyond the point where you can control your reactions. Long poker games are unnecessary in most game formats, so pause every hour and restart. Step back from the screen a bit and keep your resolve to survive the most turbulent poker times.

2. Stop reviewing results

There is nothing more destructive about a poker player's ability to focus than constantly checking his funds to investigate the effects of that last big losing hand. This is a sure way to obsess about results and to be blind to the decisions that led to them. Solid poker is about making better decisions than your opponents over and over again. The results are not only irrelevant in the short term, but distort your sense of progress as you become convinced that raising or lowering X is important while neglecting the quality of your game. Satisfying with the results is a dangerous habit that can be formed and a difficult habit to break. Try not to see your bank account more than once a week, and focus on what matters: your decisions.

3. Play within the banking system

Bad bank management is another way to make variance worse. Throwing in a higher game due to frustration and the need to reverse losses is very likely to ruin your shot. Try to have 50 buy-ins available for the next bet level before raising money or SNG games. In MTT, try to have 100-150 buy-ins available for your current participation as the variation is greater due to the larger size of the players field. Manage your bank properly to reduce variance.

4. Take on your mental problems

The fact that you enter "slope" is not a bad variation, but your reaction to it. Try writing down your three largest forms of inclination. For each one, write how the inclination is felt, what causes it, and then why this reaction is undesirable and unreasonable. Finally, write down some things you can say to yourself during the game to explain these unwanted unreasonable emotions and make sense of variation in a way that is more acceptable.

5. Avoid "balancing" long-term investments

Imagine someone pushing the pot 10 times on the flop and you are considering calling with the second best color design and two top cards. You estimate that your equity is a little less than 50%, which is also what you would need to pay there. This is a call you really don't have to make. Betting on a full stack without long-term winnings is something you should avoid to decrease game variation.

So, as a professional poker player, you are negotiating long term job stability and monthly income guaranteed by the freedom to follow your passion. I have never once regretted my choice to choose poker over a more conventional career, but that is not to say that this game is the right way to make a living for everyone who has the skills to do so. Building these skills can be a rewarding challenge in itself, even if you never quit daily work.

Marcelo Fitte's Article - https://www.pokerstars.com/espanol/blog/intellipoker/2019/pokerstars-school-10-consejos-para-manar-la-varianza-en-el-poker-180340.shtml

CHAPTER 11

The "DEAL" The AGREEMENT TIME

Players into tournament mode can eventually make it to a final table and always find it possible to make deals, which is possible on some sites such as Pokerstars, 888 Poker and others. From friends' reports, I know that many are unaware of how and when to make these deals when they eventually reach 4, 3 or 2 finalists. This is yet another moment in poker when well-applied emotional intelligence can yield a few more relevant dollars.

At this moment, feelings and emotions interfere with decisions, such as the first place in chips to overstate his ability, placing himself as a virtual champion and not agreeing to make the deal. Or fourth place at the moment, being the most skillful player in fact and not agreeing, because he has full conviction that he will beat the other opponents.

Several factors must be taken into consideration, some of which are mathematical, such as the amount of chips in each, the speed of the tournament (turbo or regular), because in turbos tournaments, the luck factor has a considerable influence on the final result and others emotional, such as each player's profile (such as playing, rock, maniac or shark), analysis of each player's technical quality (whether the player is profitable or loser) on the sites mentioned in the book and even from which region that player is playing , country in case.

These deals are attractive because the prize difference between the champion and fourth place, for example, is large. Below is a prize table for a particular tournament, where we can see that the prize difference from 3rd place to the champion is almost double.

Total prize pool: €7,500.00		Players		
		Rank ▲	Player	⊕
Current prize payout		10_LEO_MESSI_XX		
5 places paid		AdryMiamy		
		AKVENENO		
1st	€2,628.00	cmonhope		
2nd	€1,878.75	e$padaa		
3rd	€1,344.00	elchaman1986		
4th	€961.50	enroutepourlept		
5th	€687.75	Geneva_run		

Settlements are also beneficial for everyone involved in this type of dispute, as it is not every day a player arrives at the final table, so any difference in prize money can contribute to long-term profit maximization. But in a hypothetical example where a player gets to the final table every day, it would make little sense to agree but to play to win the best, because every day in this situation an experienced player will not suffer much variance (interference from the luck factor).), so with more quality in your game, will ensure maximization playing only with the mathematical factor.

Well, in practice, you don't get to the final tables on a daily basis, so all the factors we've already studied should be taken into account. In four players in this award example, some strategies in the search for DEAL are important.

1st Do not offer deal first as other players may label you as an amateur player who is afraid to gamble and lose money. It's a similar concept to playing in POSITION , or talking last.

2nd Never immediately accept agreement when you are in third position for four players in play. Even though apparently a deal in third position is advantageous, it should not be forgotten that the third placed in a moment can turn the game in one or two rounds and win the top prize. Other players should know that this possibility exists.

3rd If you are really interested in making the deal, but at the moment you are in fourth place, it is interesting to try to win some chips to improve your position by offering agreement in a better position, sometimes you can reach the lead in two or three rounds of. betting.

4th Trying to understand how important money is to other players, even online it is possible to have a parameter for this, consulting if the player is a winner or a loser, the losing player is not very worried about a difference in the prize, he wants to win to recover , in poker slang, "get out of the iron".

5th Assessing your own financial condition, if you are in a bad phase, not making the deal, and failing to win a little more, letting luck drive your winnings, can further worsen the situation and your emotional mood for the next games. It is necessary to evaluate.

6th Be patient, you are not always faced with people willing to make a deal, so if that happens, the ideal is to focus on the game and make the best decisions to win the tournament!

Remembering the importance of math x psychology in poker, if you are all in at this point, remember to offer a 40% chance to a less skilled player than you is not profitable. The opposite is, if you're facing technically superior players, don't waste 40% on beating them.

In practice there are two settlement options offered by poker platforms, but acceptance has to be for all players:

1- Chip Chop - Division based on the amount of chips each has at the time of possible agreement. If you are currently in first position, choose Chip Chop.

2- Calculation by ICM - division based on the chance of each player to win the tournament, that is, the fourth place at the moment still has the calculation of the probability of, if the game continues, of being champion, that makes to him to be attributed. a larger value. If you are in the last positions and decide to make the deal, negotiate with the other players to make it through ICM.

Let's now look at a possible agreement in our example.

If there was a Deal in this award structure, one could come up with something like:

1st € 2.400.00

2nd € 1 . 750 .00

3rd € 1 . 522 .00

4 € 1,139 .00

If I were in first place at the moment, I would accept, as I would be earning € 228.00 less to guarantee a possible difference of € 1666.50 if I was fourth in the course of play, with only 4 players being possible in only three or

Four rounds happen turns, especially if the tournament structure is turbo, when the blinds go up quickly.

On some platforms, after Deal, the game ends and on others, the game proceeds with the award already settled. In all settlement situations you can chat in the universal language in English.

CHAPTER 12

ROI - RETURN OBTAINED ON INVESTMENT

Many people do not know where the profit comes from or where the loss of a poker player goes. It is common to hear comments that a particular site took all money from a particular player , as it is not known that poker sites do not earn money from the player, only the provision of the software or application service. A poker player's profit comes from the defeat of other poker players. Now it's easy to imagine where a poker player's profit comes from, most of who play hobby poker , or who don't improve on the game and can't win at the levels they practice.

Knowing exactly what your ROI is, how it is calculated and how it can affect your profitability is essential for any poker player. We offer you a detailed analysis.

ROI stands for "return on investment" and is essentially a tournament player's way of keeping track of results. We may be familiar with the idea that cash game players control their own winning rate using BB / 100, ie the amount of big blinds won divided by an average of 100 hands.

Unfortunately, this does not work very well as a measure of a tournament player's win rate. Why? Because it could have a positive BB / 100 win rate but lose money overall due to rising blind levels. It is possible to earn more bbs than our opponents in a Sit & Go or tournament, but not yet finish in the top.

Therefore, tournament and Sit & Go players clearly need a different method of controlling winnings. That's where the ROI comes in.

How to calculate ROI

The ROI formula is very simple.

$$\frac{Overall\ Profits}{Amount\ spent\ on\ Buyins}$$

* as a decimal - multiply by 100 to get ROI percentage

By deducting the tournament lockers from our tournament winnings we will have our total profit. That is, we have to subtract the lockers from the gain totals to calculate our net profit.

Tip: The result will be a decimal format and must be multiplied by 100 to get our ROI percentage.

Let's practice with some examples to see if the formula makes sense.

Example 1. We played 100 $ 1.00 Sit & Gos. Our gross earnings are $ 256.00 (not profit, gross earnings). What is our ROI?

See if you can answer the question by calculating your ROI. Then check the answer with the calculation below.

Tip: When we talk about "gross profit", we are talking about all the money we make, regardless of losses and lockers paid.

Answer: The first step is to calculate the profit. We probably made it a little harder than it really is. If we knew our starting balance, we could simply look at our current balance and find our net income.

Anyway, in this scenario, we invested $ 100 in lockers (100 x $ 1.00). So if our gross earnings are $ 256, that means our net income is $ 156.

Total Profit = $ 156.00

Amount spent on lockers - $ 100

156/100 = 1.56

So keep in mind that this value is our ROI expressed as a decimal. We can multiply this number by 100 if we prefer to see our ROI as a percentage. In this case, the ROI% would be 156%.

So basically, every time we play one of those $ 1.00 Sit & Go tournaments, we're getting an average of 156% of our stakes, which is $ 1.56. This result is a huge absolute return on investment. A reasonable ROI would be around 10% over a significant sample.

Example 2. We played 1000 $ 5.00 Sit & Gos with a 13% ROI. What is the total profit? What are our gross earnings?

Gross earnings are practically useless; As players, we are only interested in net income. But calculating gross earnings will help ensure that we understand the ROI formula and that we know the difference between gross earnings and total (net) profit.

Again, see if you can answer the question and then check your answer with the calculation below.

Answer: If we have a 13% ROI over this sample, it essentially means that for every $ 5.00 we invest, we are getting an additional 13% of our $ 5.00 clout. So how much is 13% of $ 5.00?

$ 5.00 x 0.13 = $ 0.65.

So for each of the 1000 tournaments played, we got an average of $ 0.65. So what is our total profit?

$ 0.65 x 1000 = $ 650

However, our gross earnings will include the amount spent on the lockers. In this case, we spend $ 5,000 on lockers (1,000 x $ 5). Thus, our gross earnings would be $ 5,650, which means that our gross losses would therefore be $ 5,000, since we know that our net income is $ 650.

Sometimes when calculating, it may be helpful to do a bit of reverse engineering just to help us check the numbers. Let's see if we can enter the numbers into the ROI formula to get back to the initial 13% ROI.

$$\frac{Overall\ Profits}{Amount\ spent\ on\ Buyins}$$

So the total profits were $ 650.00.

We spent $ 5,000 on lockers.

Our ROI expressed as a decimal is 650/5000 = 0.13.

We can multiply this number by 100 to reach our original 13% ROI.

ROI and variance

Perhaps one of the reasons for having an extremely high ROI value in the first example was the very small sample size. We had only played 100 Sit & Go tournaments.

That number may seem high, but if we play less than about 200 Sit & Go, our ROI can be extremely inaccurate. Sit & Gos swings can last over a few hundred tournaments.

This is a tricky issue, especially as we start playing at larger events such as MTTs. The more participants in each of the tournaments we enter, the greater the variance and the larger sample size required to achieve a somewhat accurate ROI.

How to maximize ROI

In many cases, we want to maximize our ROI when playing in tournaments.

We can maximize our ROI:

Playing in networks with low tournament fees.

Looking for networks with quiet tournament games .

However, ROI is not the most important factor for a tournament player. A high ROI can give us bragging rights; but for professional players , the most important metric is usually $ / h (dollars per hour).

We may find, for example, that if we play in faster format Sit & Gos (faster structure and blind levels etc.), our ROI will be lower. But if we're making more dollars per hour playing in these formats, does it really matter that our total ROI is lower?

The same can be said for upper limit Sit & Gos. It is true that we can maximize our ROI by playing lower limit Sit & Gos, but our hourly rate is higher in larger betting games. Maybe we shouldn't worry so much about our slightly lower ROI.

After all, ultimately, ROI can be used as a good general guide to determining how we are doing in tournaments. But we must also remember that ROI is strongly affected by variance. In many cases, it will not be the most important metric in determining a tournament player's success.

"Class A" players are estimated to have 30% to 60% ROI in multi - table tournaments .

A regular mid-level or even weak player earns a ROI of around 10% to 25% in multi-table tournaments.

At cash game tables it is estimated that the profit of a "class A" player at NL25 + is around 4bb per 100bb.

The following is a graph of a class A cash game player:

Below is a class "A" player chart from multi-table tournaments:

Note that the profitability of the cash game player has little variance, ie few periods of losses, but remember that you are a "class A" player.

Tournament player profitability has more variance, loss periods, even being a "class A" player, because in tournaments, as already mentioned in this book, on average only 10% of players are awarded in tournaments, ie In many tournaments a good player doesn't even get into the money, but because he is an above average player, when he reaches the finals of another tournament, he tends to make the expected profit.

Below is a graph of a "class B" player in tournaments, note that you are a profitable player, but you increase your profits very slowly.

Gráfico de um jogador nível "B"

CHAPTER 13

THE TIME OF TRUTH, WHAT YOU CAN REALLY WIN IN POKER

Chances are you were very excited about the poker player profitability charts from the previous chapter. But you must you bring a bad news , it is unlikely that you come to a similar chart, because it is estimated that only 5% of poker players come to results like those, and that a portion of 70% is losing player, not disparaging these, it may be those who play for fun and are not too concerned about results financial game .

Anyone who often plays live poker with friends or in poker clubs may realize this, there are always 1 or 2 players who always make it to the final table, that would be 5%, some make it to some final tables and win something, 5 or more. 6, and the rest, which would be 70%, almost never make it to the final table. Clearly, they are players who lose money in profitability, but they can still be happy to play poker because they must be part of that group who play only for fun or hobby.

The good news is that this book is aimed at the 25% of poker practically, who are those who make a profit, without devoting 100% of their time and investment in poker, are the players who have an extra income in poker and also as a hobby. Once on my YouTube channel (COAST POKER BRAZIL), launched a mini project for my subscribers, was the " S eja a lucrative recreational player" , perhaps those 25% of poker practitioners fit this project ...

The chapters dealing with the profitability of the poker game are suitable for this group of players, guiding how to make money in poker, even if you are not a "A" player.

To be able to reach that goal in poker and be part of this portion of players, it is essential to follow the advice of the next chapters, because if you do not, you risk going out of the 25% range and entering the majority in the 70%. losing players.

If you are reading this book, I believe the goal is to reach the positive goal of poker.

If your interest is not financial, take the opportunity to improve your knowledge and develop skills in emotional intelligence, present in this game.

If you can develop any technique and practice in poker, I believe that even if it is not your priority, you will be among those who make some money in poker, which is the reward for dedication, as in any other financial activity.

CHAPTER 14

THE TRUTH ABOUT ONLINE POKER PLATFORMS

You may wonder why we will once again approach the profits of a poker platform if you are a player and not an owner of a poker club or game application. One reason is to make it clear why a legitimate online poker platform, I mean those licensed, as explained in the chapter on the legality of poker, would have no intention of breaking or "stealing" their players. Instead, they invest millions of dollars in security and measures to protect their customers, us players.

What happens are operators' strategies to maximize their profits, such as building lucrative tournament structures for them. In a turbo tournament , for example , the entry profit is faster because tournaments last less time, so players who are eliminated go to other modalities or other tournaments generating more rake . We can not criticize the operators for increasing their profitability, because many actions are taken to satisfy another part of customers. As in the example above about turbos tournaments, there are many players who like it because it takes less time, and not all players can spend 6 or 8 hours playing a day-to-day tournament. In the next chapters, some advice will be given on choosing the right structures and tables for your purpose.

One more reason is that the secret to making money in poker even if you are not a "class A" player is to join platforms or rooms that offer generous VIP programs, in practice the best VIP programs pay regular players the so-called "RAKEBACK". , remembering that rake is the service fee that the platform charges to offer software and services to players (it's their profit) and rakeback is the return of a portion of the rake they earn, ie it's a customer loyalty agreement. customers .

Thus, an online poker platform will only be able to offer a rakeback deal to its customers, only if they are profitable, as some of their profits will go back to the rakeback player.

Example:

The same player who plays an average of 1000 $ 11 tournaments per month pays $ 1 rake per rake tournament, generating a total of $ 1000 monthly rake to the site. There are currently reliable platforms that offer rakeback deals around 35%, so in this example the player in that deal would get 35% of the $ 1000, which would be $ 350 cash rakeback . (In later chapters you will be shown how to get these rakeback deals). Note, even if this player made no profit in the 1000 tournaments played, he would win the same $ 350 rakeback.

CHAPTER 15

DIFFERENCES BETWEEN RAKEBACK AND BONUS

As explained earlier rakeback is the return of part of the rake paid to the poker room for the service, the famous tournament fees. Usually these deals are not offered on the main pages of the sites, they are offered by business partners who create poker content, such as the portal www.litoralpoker.com . It is not very advantageous for the poker platform to offer these deals very clearly, as rakeback deals usually have no expiration date, ie it is a promotion that usually has no expiration date, in a quasi "LIFE TIME" model. . But changes in agreements are not prohibited and platforms do. We have seen cases of rakeback programs ending in most major poker rooms, such as Pokerstars and 888Poker. In these two specific rooms, the generous rakeback programs have been replaced by less expensive financial programs and replaced by bonuses. It should be noted that it is better to participate in a change in plans with large rooms than not to receive rakeback in the event of unreliable room failure.

The Poker Bonus is nonetheless a rakeback, as the site gives a bonus amount that is part of the profit the player has given him, ie a part of the rake. The difference is that the bonus usually has an expiration date, for example: 100% first deposit bonus that needs to be withdrawn within sixty or ninety days. And the bonus usually only comes into account as the player is playing and generating rake, ie shows to be a valid rakeback. Some platforms, such as Pokertars and 888Poker, after discontinuing the aforementioned VIP program have opted in to insert intermediate deposit bonuses, not only on the first deposit. Often some players receive email with the bonus announcement in their account, such as "deposit $ 60 or more and earn $ 15". Bonuses are good anyway, so take advantage of opportunities when available.

Some players have already asked the author which option to select when joining a new platform when the choice is available and the answer 98% of the time is the choice of rakeback simply because it is indefinite. Although in most cases, by opening the account on the site, the player will have the first deposit bonus and at least one traditional VIP plan in force.

In the following chapters, you will be mentioned how to choose your rakeback and bonus deals with Litoral Poker.

CHAPTER 1 6

MAIN DIFFERENCES BETWEEN CASH GAME ET ORNEIOS

In the chapter on poker player profitability, it was quite clear that the profit is higher at cash game tables, than at tournaments, in the graphics, you can see the difference, not only in amount but also in variation.

Platforms profit is also much higher at cash game tables, because the service fee charged, the rake, is per pot played, in other words per game played, while in tournaments you pay the entry fee to play. an event that can take hours.

Even so it is important to be clear that the choice of the game to play will depend on many factors, one of them is the ability or profile of each player, or even their satisfaction. If a player feels comfortable or happy to play tournaments, it would not be advisable to change the game, just for the reason that the other is more lucrative. One can come across even with a reverse result, instead of earning more, the player breaks and the times to give up playing.

Cash game tables are recommended for those players who don't have much time available, playing a few hours a week with a good rakeback deal, like Betfair Poker (35%) or Black Chip Poker (27%) would have to have considerable return in this mode.

Maybe the differences aren't even financial between ring game and tournament play, there are emotional factors that can often make a difference at the time of choice.

In tournaments you always have the title of champion, the participation of a final table etc.

At the cash game tables, the excitement gives way to the real money win, because those who make the most money out of a game session may come out with the title of best player at the table, but it is quite different from a big tournament with more than 1000 participants for example.

In short, one should never choose one mode or another, because of the financial factor, satisfaction and comfort zone make much difference in long term results. Since no one plays poker for a fixed amount of time, it is important to consider this emotional factor.

CHAPTER 17

RAKEBACK REFLECTIONS AND COMPENSATIONS IN FINAL RESULT

According to the previous information, one can reach the conclusion that the benefit of rakeback has no negative point, because even if a player win not playing at the tables, the amount of rakeback will be guaranteed, as it is independent of the result s as it is a part the service charge of the site that returns to the player, and the player pays service fee when he wins or loses at the tables.

We will have direct consequences on the result in three situations on the result of the beneficiaries of the rakeback program.

Situation # 1 - The player gets an above-average positive ROI, that is, the profitability of a class A player and with the sum of rakeback, further improves his final income.

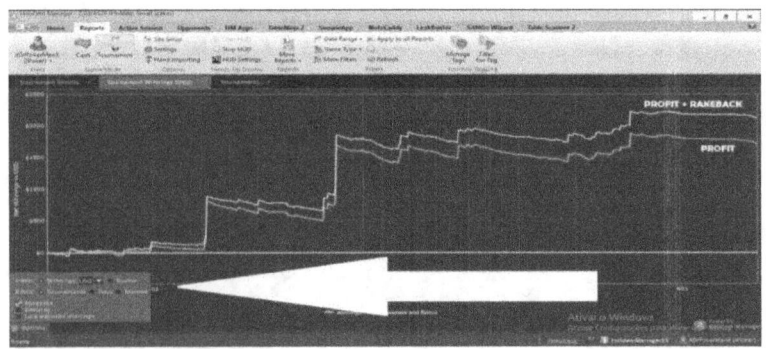

The green line is the positive result in a series of 450 tournaments played. The yellow line is the result added to the rakeback. In the following chapters you will be exposed how to configure the reporting software.

Situation # 2 - The player gets a positive ROI or almost zero to zero, without profits, without prejudice, where the rakeback ends up generating a minimum profit or a considered profit (as graph below) , nothing fairer, because the player must have spent minimum time during sessions.

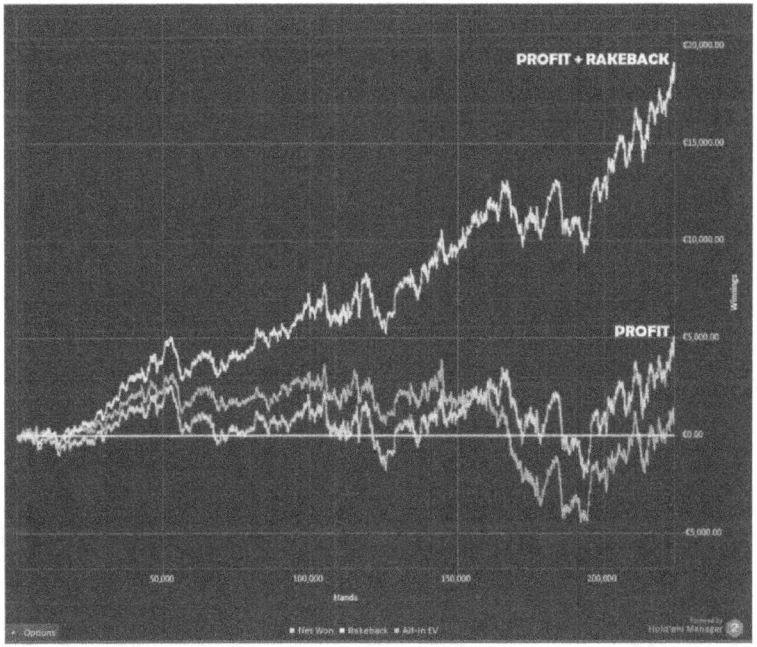

In the graph above, the result with the sum of rakeback is represented by the yellow line. You can see that this player was very close to the zero line, representing the result of the games on the green line.

Situation # 3 - The player goes through a bad phase and a bitter injury and with the rakeback performance can be almost zero to zero.

In the graph above the negative result is represented by the green line and the blue line represents the result with the sum of the rakeback.

In the chart below, the player would have been in red, but with rakeback, still made some profit!

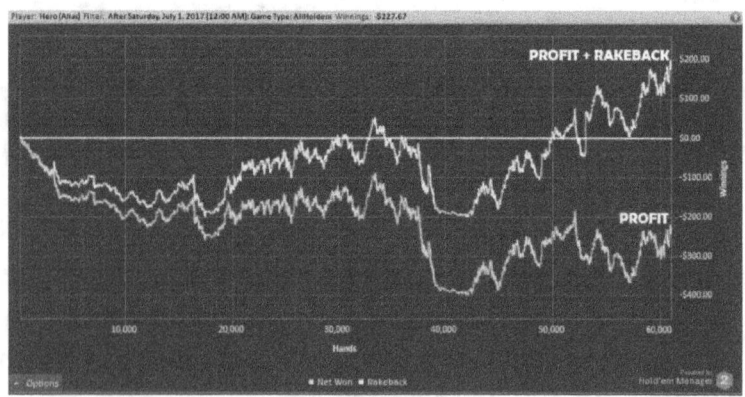

In addition to the reflexes on the results in the three situations above, we find other situations that players can compensate for some losses, such as the exchange loss . Few players realize that they always buy chips with currency variation plus a service charge from credit operators and when they sell their credits, they pay that fee again, with currency difference. It is normal for these exchange rates to be charged in countries where the platform currency is different from the local currency, such as Brazil that has the Real currency and most sites use either the dollar or euro as their primary currency. Porting rakeback can still help offset these losses.

CHAPTER 1 8

CHOOSE FROM THE DIFFERENT ONLINE POKER PLATFORMS AVAILABLE

As discussed in chapter 2 of this book , where the theme was the legality of poker in Brazil and around the world. Again, the first criterion for choosing an online poker room or platform today is credibility, which has as its main seal operating licenses with the governing bodies of online gambling in the world. In a way, we can give more credibility to the poker platforms and poker rooms that are licensed in the United States.

Currently the most well-known sites, Pokerstars, Full Tilt, 888 Poker, Partypoker, Black Chip Poker (WPN), Americas Card Room (WPN), Ya Poker (WPN) and Betfair Poker (Ipoker) operate legally in the USA.

More information about the mentioned rooms can be found at www.litoralpoker.com.br

A classic example of this view is that the poker player for a while, sometimes for years, on a given platform, can make some money, but suddenly the platform goes bankrupt and this player loses everything he has won , plus one. capital. This example is very real, even happened a few times.

Of the trusted platforms, they all have some appeal, be it a generous rakeback program, great customer service or great software, as in the case of Pokerstars, which even when drastically reduced its VIP program, still managed to maintain much of its field. , due to the quality of its almost unbeatable service and software. Almost, because in the last two years, virtually all platforms have updated their software and managed to get very close to the quality of Pokerstars, which has always been unanimous on this requirement.

In the characteristics that influence the choice decision, we come to the VIP benefits, the rakeback programs, which is certainly determinant, as your choice comes straight to your box.

Importantly, one of the ways to protect your capital is to keep it spread in two or three rooms, so in addition to security issues, you can still narrow your variance a little. This is one of the reasons that Litoral Poker Brazil is opening accounts on all of the trusted platforms mentioned above and one of them may offer the benefit of differentiated rakeback, such as Betfair Poker (35% VIP plus rakeback) and Black Chip Poker (27% rakeback and VIP Elite benefits).

One of the latest news was the creation of the European shared market between Portugal, France and Spain for POKERSTARS. ES The most interesting and intriguing thing is that they are accepting players from other regions, a fact that should not persist for a long time, as there is little point in having two equal sites accepting players from all over the world. Although the Pokertars have reduced their rakeback program, it is advantageous to play in the European market because of the tournament structures have greater playability, the games are in euros, plus d and a very soft field. At Litoral Poker you can open an account, and even for those who already have a Pokerstars.com account, you can open another one.

More information about the mentioned rooms can be found at www.litoralpoker.com.br

PROMOCODE BLACK CHIP POKER: **litoralpoker**

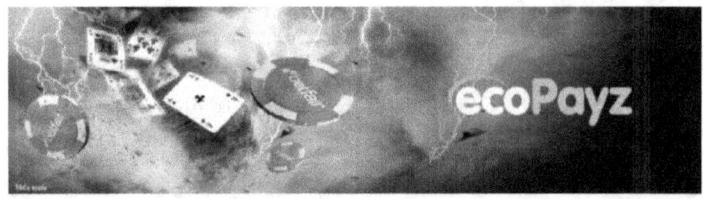

CHAPTER 1 9

REGISTERING ON PLATFORMS AND KNOWING SOME MODES

As already said where to find the VIP benefits of online poker, www.litoralpoker.com .

Now let's show how, as many players go directly to the platforms and open their accounts, they lose the chance of the best rakeback or bonus deals, as mentioned earlier, the platforms do not offer the best deals on the main page of their sites as it is a showcase for generic and non-special customers who open their accounts with the help of a trading partner such as Litoral Poker Brazil.

First step:

Access the site www.litoralpoker.com.br and after

Access the BONUS tab in the top menu:

Second step:

Just click on the banners of the sites, you will be redirected directly to the platforms and linked offers by Litoral Poker Brazil.

On this page you'll always have the best poker market promotions available on the most trusted platforms, as well as the digital wallets that serve for deposit and withdrawal on the sites, payouts and receipts will be covered in the next chapter!

On some platforms, to enter the main page of the site, already have an option to register, and then you do download the poker software, as Betfair Poker , PokerStars , PartyPoker .

3 pasos fáciles para comenzar a jugar en PokerStars

After opening accounts or trying VIP benefits on existing accounts, sign up (litoralpoker.com homepage

After opening the account on the platform you will find the various game modes to play, in general the game offerings are similar in all poker applications.

Let's get to know some PokerStars.es (Spain) games now:

MULTI-TABLE TOURNAMENTS:

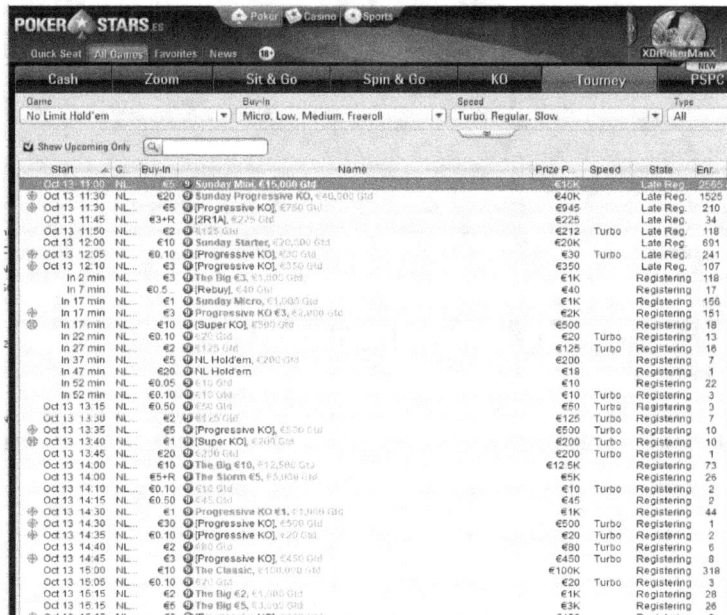

In the Pokerstars lobby, we are in the mode most wanted by most players, the multi-table tournaments, better known as "MTT". Each line in the lobby is a tournament available for registration, with important information such as start time, entry fee, BUY-IN, tournament name, blind level speed, REGULAR or TURBO (regular tournaments have estimated time between 5 and 8 hours, while the turbos last a maximum of 5 hours), the number of players at the moment and the status of the tournament, which can be: announced (at a future date), registering (starting in a few days) hours), late registration (it has already started, but you can still log in, usually late registrations on PokerStars are 1 hour for turbos tournaments and 2 hours for regular tournaments).

CHARACTERISTICS OF THE TOURNAMENT MODE:

It's more popular because it's the opportunity to turn pennies into jackpots as it brings together many players who contribute to the formation of the prize pool.

This is the most controlled way to play poker, as the player only loses the amount paid for the entry in each record, even if you buy back or additional chips, it is easier to control investments, especially for novice players.

In both online and live games, it is an opportunity to tackle various player profiles, even from different cultures when they are from different countries , due to the high number of opponents in a single tournament.

Guaranteed prize tournaments, usually stated in the name (30K GTD), are tournaments that guarantee a minimum prize pool. When a service operator (poker site) offers these tournaments, it is almost certain that the number of entries required for the formation of the prize will be reached, as it would not be normal for an operator to always complete the prize amount as it would tend to "break or fail ".

CASH GAME TABLES

The CASH GAME table is a single-table form of play, in which the chips in play represent cash values, meaning that if the player wins $ 10.00 in chips in a pot, he will be winning $ 10 if he loses as well.

Tables are defined by the value of the blinds at the table $ 01.00 - $ 0.02 means that the BIG BLIND mandatory bet is $ 0.02. Usually the minimum required to sit at the table is 50 to 100 Bigblinds, ie at a $ 0.02 cash game table, the minimum to sit is to buy from $ 1.00 to $ 2.00.

One of the advantages of cash games is that the player can leave at will, unlike tournaments that cannot be withdrawn until it is eliminated or the tournament is over. So for people who want to play poker with little time available, it can be an opportunity.

The author of the book strongly recommends poker beginners who choose to play the cash game tables, as these tables have a high number of experienced and professional players, even at the lower limits, being single table games, the caster of players is smaller, unlike tournaments.

Another considerable advantage is the format of commissions paid to the operator, usually 5% of each pot played, unlike tournaments that are paid only for the buy-in. On the other hand, if you choose to earn income on "RAKEBACK" you can make a reasonable profit too, because if you pay more commission to the site (operator) you will have more "commission back" (RAKEBACK).

Some pro players spend hours playing home games, without winning or losing at the tables, but make a good profit on RAKEBACK. For this reason, there are many professional players in this sport.

One the big difference of the cash game of games is that the blinds do not rise, that is, the table where the big blind is $ 0.02, and the player remains at this table for an hour or more, the big blind will always be $ 0.02. This way players never come under the pressure of increasing blinds, as in tournaments. Risky play due to blind pressure does not exist in cash games, so this is important information when a novice player faces an experienced player at the tables.

SPIN AND GO

Spin & Go's are the fastest way to earn up to 10,000 times your buy-in. Available for Hold'em and Omaha, Spin & Go's have randomly awarded prizes and give you a chance to win up to $ 1,000,000 in minutes. And with $ 0.25 buy-ins, it's the exciting poker format anyone can play!

How Spin & Go Works

Spin & Go are fast-paced 3-Max Hyper-Turbo Sit & Go tournaments with 500 starting stacks. Tournaments have randomly drawn prizes that award between two and 12,000 times the buy-in, with prizes of up to $ 1,000,000 to be won.

Omaha Spin & Go games play out like regular versions of these exciting tournaments, with the only difference that the game played is Omaha instead of Texas Hold'em. In Omaha, each player is dealt four hole cards and must use exactly two of them to make their poker hand. To learn more about this fun and action-packed variant, see here.

To get started, select your buy-in and the number of simultaneous tournaments you wish to play and click the ' Register' button . It is so easy! You will be seated at a tournament table until two other players register.

Once a third player signs up for your Spin & Go tournament, there will be a random draw to decide the size of the tournament's prize pool. The spinner in the center of the table will display the prize for all players.

The first leg will be dealt and the Spin & Go prize will be up for grabs!

Example: You sign up for a $ 3 Spin & Go. After two other players have registered, the prize will be randomly drawn and announced to players before the first card is dealt. The first place prize will be multiplied between two and 10,000 times your buy-in, which means you can turn $ 3 into $ 6 to $ 30,000!

Most Spin and Go's are played as 'winner-take-all' tournaments, except when your Spin & Go reaches one of the three highest prize levels. In these Spin & Go, no player leaves empty handed, as second and third places also receive 10% of the first place prize.

Structure

We offer Spin & Go's in a selection of different buy-ins as shown above. Regardless of the buy-in, players will start the tournament with 500 chips and play three-minute levels. It is not possible to do business at Spin & Go's.

Awards and Odds

Multiplicador do Prêmio	Prêmio Spin & Go de primeiro lugar de US $ 0,25	Prêmio Spin & Go de US $ 1 em Primeiro Lugar	Prêmio Spin & Go de US $ 3 em Primeiro Lugar	Frequência
12.000	$ 2.500	US $ 10.000	$ 30.000	1 em 1.000.000
240	$ 50	$ 200	$ 600	30 em 1.000.000
120	$ 25	$ 100	$ 300	75 em 1.000.000
25	US $ 6.25	$ 25	$ 75	1.000 em 1.000.000
10	US $ 2.50	$ 10	$ 30	5.000 em 1.000.000
5	US $ 1.25	$ 5	$ 15	85.000 em 1.000.000
3	US $ 0.75	$ 3	$ 9	414.012 em 1.000.000
2	US $ 0.50	$ 2	$ 6	494.882 em 1.000.000

8% do buy-in vai para o rake

Opening Your BetFair Poker Account

BetFair Poker Tournament Lobby

Opening your Partypoker account:

On other platforms, such as Black Chip Poker and 888Poker , the main page of the site does not open the account, only downloads the poker application and opens the account when you first open the application.

Opening Your 888poker Account

After downloading, install the app and when it first opens, register your account and open it.

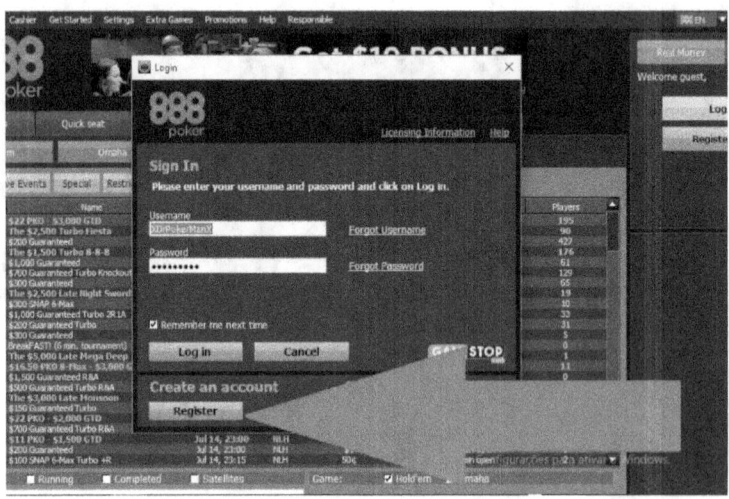

888 Poker Tournament Lobby

Opening Your Black Chip Poker Account

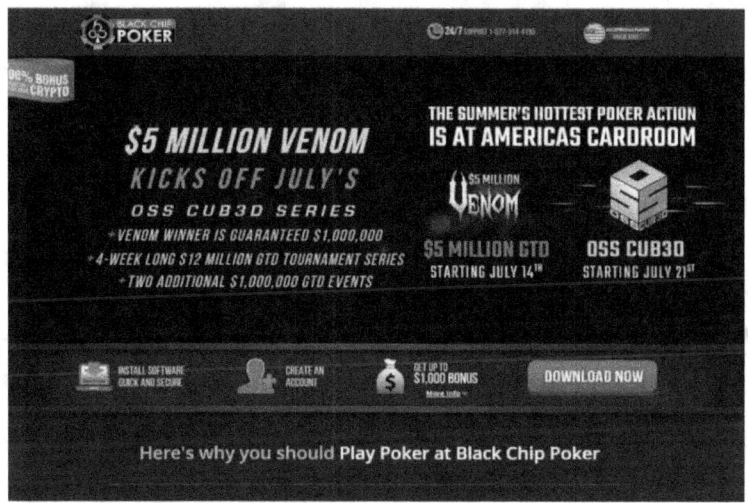

USE PROMOCODE: <u>litoralpoker</u>

Black Chip Poker Tournament Lobby

VERY IMPORTANT!

If you already have an account with no benefit platform, never try to open a second account . Having more than one account on behalf of the same user is prohibited. With the exception of POKERTARS.COM and POKERSTARS.ES

We online poker players always look for safe and reliable platforms, and one of the security criteria is not to allow a player to have more than one account in their name, or even two accounts in different names that are used from the same address or computer.

If you are in a similar situation, please contact us or initially register at the link on the homepage of www.litoralpoker.com.br

WOULD YOU LIKE TO CHANGE YOUR NICK NAME ON SOME PLATFORM?

Some players try to open a second account on some site because they want to change their table nickname and it ends up in the irregular situation we mentioned above.

What can be done is to open an account on another site of the same network, managed to open the account and will continue playing on the same platform, in the case of Black Chip Poker and Americas Card Room.

The possibility of Pokerstar.es European market is also very interesting, you can open an account on "Pokerstars" with another Nick, but in this case the games will be from the European field, not bad!

Also use this option if you already have an account on the platforms, registering the data with us, we will try the VIP benefits, even if the account is not opened with us. This option is valid on Betfair Poker, Partypoker, Ecopayz, Neteller or Skrill.

https://litoralpoker.com.br/cadastros.html

CHAPTER 20

SUPPORT SOFTWARE FOR REPORTING OF RESULTS AND WEBSITES

First and foremost , we need to remember how to measure poker results, as many confuse the absolute values of winnings with profit with return on investment (ROI). So one should look at ROI first, because it is no use for a player to earn $ 1 billion in total prize money, having invested $ 2 billion over a period of time . Any positive ROI, 5%, 10%, 20% 40%, 60% should be considered satisfactory, because the higher the invested amounts, the ROI tends to fall, as 5% profit of $ 1 million is $ 50. thousand. Each player must choose the conditions that are best suited for them, from availability of working capital (bankroll) to availability of time to practice, because this relationship is part of the economic cog, if you can invest less money with more time or more capital in less time.

Most online poker players already know about the supporting software, commonly known as HUD, the most popular and used are Holdem Manager 2 and Poker Tracker with their respective updates. These software support both game time and post game play analysis as well as profitability assessment and results such as ROI, rakeback, etc. It is good to note that this year 2019, some platforms, like Partypoker are placing restrictions on the use of these software, in order to make the game fairer, since a user who plays with hud takes some advantage against who does not play, even who not being able to put it either, but for the complexity they give up. In the last update of Black Chip Poker, there were also restrictions, but until July 2019, the ban was not made official. There is a possibility that most rooms will ban their use in a short time. But as has not been defined, in this chapter we will put a mini tutorial on how to configure rakeback information in Hold Manager 2, and in other similar software, the procedure is very similar. Remembering that using this software for analysis does not alter gain or performance, it is only for gain control, the earned values entered into the poker platform and not in the supporting software, if you do not use, you do not have to worry about any interference. in its rakeback profitability.

At www.litoralpoker.com.br you can also purchase the software in the BONUS tab.

After opening the software, click on "Settings"

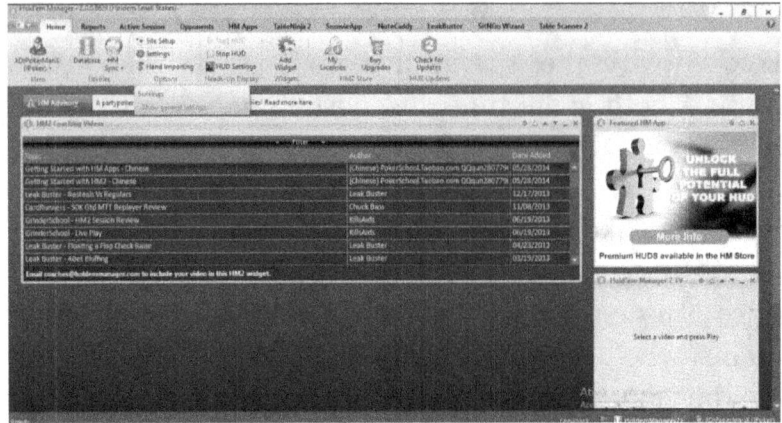

Select the Rakeback and Bonuses option, press "+" to add a rakeback agreement you have on the specific platform.

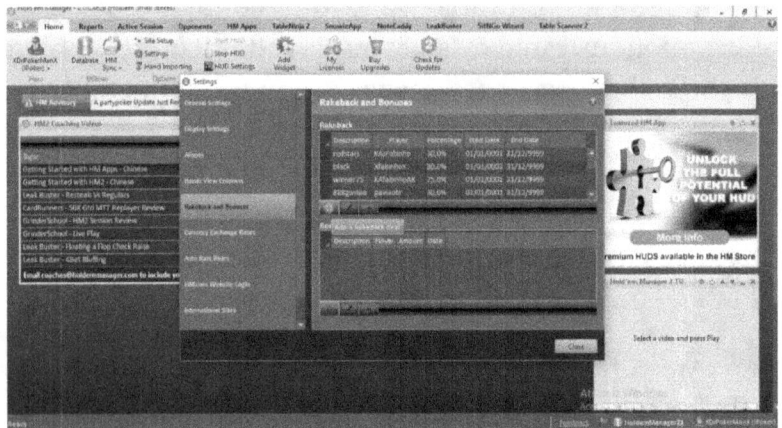

Name this deal, if I put TEST, enter the percentage of the deal, on the test I put 35%, hit the Select button, it will look like a box for you to select the player who has the rakeback on the selected platform.

If you want to register your Betfair player, who is from the Ipoker network, you should look for your Betfair player nick, this is if the hud has already filed a hand history from that player on the site.

Hit ok and you're done!

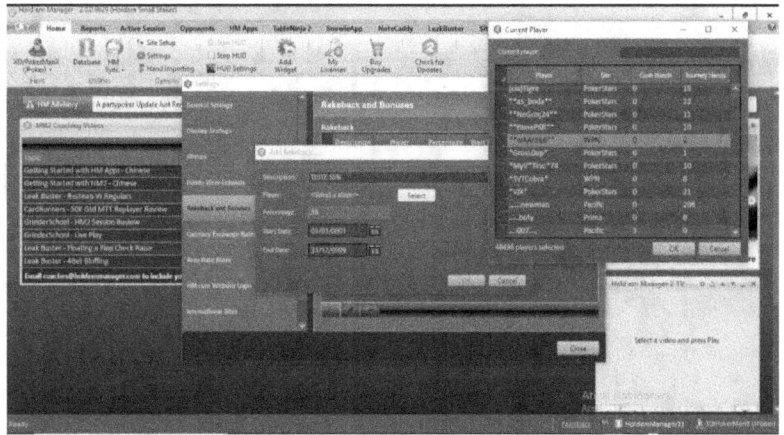

Now let's see how you configure rakeback to appear in the result graphs.

Go back to the main lobby of the software and hit "Reports" which means reports, for Tournament, use the filter with dates, entry values and so on.

Opening both cash game and tournament graphics, go to the "options" button in the lower left corner and check the rakeback option. The yellow line representing the final result plus the configured rakeback will appear, 35% of Betfair for example.

Again, this report is for information only; if not done, the platform agreed rakeback will be credited in the same way.

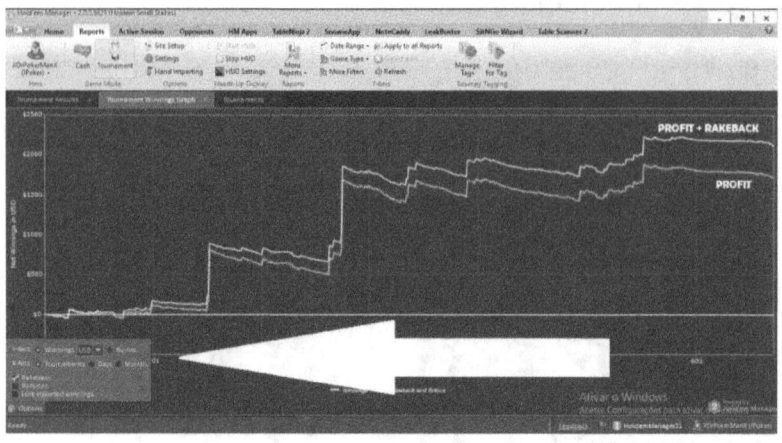

20 .1 Analyzing Your Web Site Results

In addition to setting up software to analyze financial results, you can also make this assessment through websites such as: www.sharkscope.com and www.pokerprolabs.com . But not all poker platforms report their results to specialized sites and you need to authorize or block the submission of this information. When released, you can see your own results and the numbers of your opponents, such as number of matches played, total absolute profit or loss, and the percentage of ROI (return on investment). It is important to be aware of some variations from one website to another, as they have different filters and some methods that differ, but generally reflect the reality of the result.

Below is how the results are presented at www.sharkscope.com :

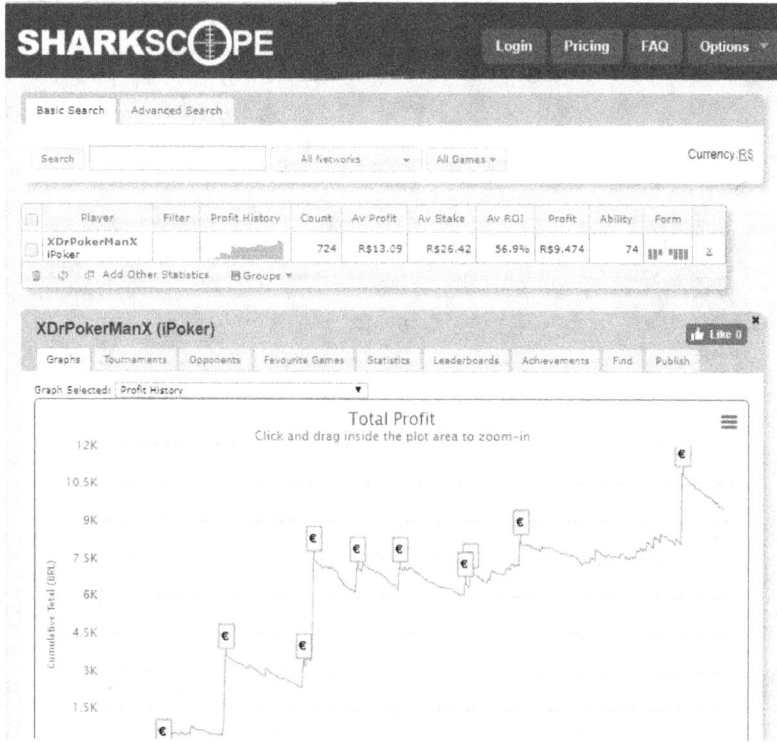

All are presented with a graph that serves to have a quick assessment, if any player is profitable or loser, so when playing, just check the results of opponents for decision making. The tip is to use this information in final tournament stages, as it is not very useful in the early stages, and is usually very useful in semi-final and final tables.

Below is how the results are presented at https://pokerprolabs.com :

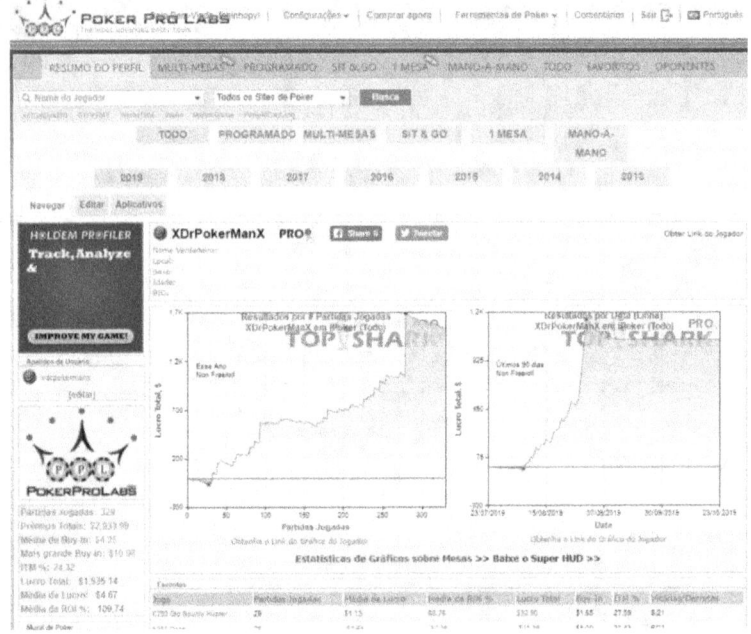

One more important detail, in this form of consultation it is not possible to know the gain of the player in RAKEBACK, as in the configuration in supporting software.

These services are offered through monthly or yearly subscriptions, but all offer some free and limited use, so if the user has no intention of subscribing, they can make some consultations without any payment.

Chapter 21 - ASPECTS OF TAX Profit The TIVIADE online poker

Perhaps one of the most important chapters of this book is now beginning, as it not only shows the effects of taxation on poker player profitability, but is well intertwined with the legal aspects of poker, especially in Brazil.

In the chapter dealing with the legality of poker in Brazil, it was very clear that its practice and even its commercialization was no longer a crime or an illegal act, as until a few years ago. However, it was also explained that despite a non-criminal act, there is still a certain kind of prejudice against poker because it remains an unregulated sport. In Brazil there was the regulation of football through the "Pelé Law", many must have heard, is the law that regulates the contracts of soccer players and marketing of soccer in Brazil. Poker regulation may occur alongside the law that should release casinos in Brazil soon, but until that happens, we will have to use some accounting knowledge to deal with the following issues.

Assuming that a player, without necessarily being a "class A" player, receives in his bank accounts in banks in Brazil monthly, on average about $ 200, today equivalent to $ 760.00. At first glance not much attention is given, because in Brazil income up to R $ 2500,00 are exempt from Income Tax. The problem is that this same player who has only an extra income in poker, has other activities that generates an average monthly income of approximately $ 4800.00. Adding that in, we would have the total of $ 5,560 on average deposited in this recreational poker player's account that has an extra income in poker.

Well, few people know that deposits over R $ 5000.00 per month in bank accounts in Brazil, are now monitored by the Central Bank and consequently, the information can be passed on to the IRS. In other countries they should have devices similar to ours.

The worst can happen in the following years, this player now as a taxpayer, in the period of the previous year's Income Tax Declaration, does not even consider informing the receipts of the R $ 760.00 monthly in his account, because, neither, these amounts. were all poker profits, entered the account, but not necessarily would be profits, as this player may have spent about $ 400, invested these amounts in tournament entries, so your average profit would be around $ 360.00, typical of a recreational poker player. In this regard, perhaps one of the only drawbacks of the poker game continues without a regulation in Brazil, because it prevents shoot down expenses in the game D eclaraç will of income tax, which can fit in the income tax exemption range. This taxpayer would risk having to pay taxes on the total amount of monthly bank entries, about R $ 5,560.00, if not declared in the subsequent year, would still risk being fined as well. That is, even a small profit in poker could cause complications with the IRS for lack of better management, which will be covered in the next chapters.

What also happens constantly is that the player earns values on a particular site, tries to sell his credits quickly, gets local currency in his bank and ends up buying credits to play on other sites. Then the negative impact on profitability may be even worse, because he received the amounts that were not even spent, were invested in other platforms and would have to be declared subject to tax. Note that tax reflexes can be dire even for low-income, recreational players or those who only have an extra income in poker. These tax consequences may be much worse for "class A" players who receive current account amounts at Brazilian banks far beyond the tax-free ranges.

That's right, "class A" players can have disastrous tax complications. In Spain we had an example of this in 2011, Francisco Vallejo Pons one of the leading names in Spanish chess, having received the title of Grandmaster at 16 years. In 2011, he began his career in online poker and made over € 1 million in prizes. Even with this high value earned, was a victim of variance and ended the nano with a small loss. Spanish law at the time, however, stated that the total amount of premiums should be taxed, not the balance. The Spanish government subsequently charged more than € 500,000, about $ 2 million, based on the old law, similar to Brazilian tax law in 2019. In 2012 the Spanish law came to change and solved future problems in these aspects.

Returning to Brazil, in live poker the problems can also be catastrophic, suppose the player who spent about $ 3,000 a month (with buy-in, transportation, food and lodging) on live tournaments, spending about R $ 24,000 a year, and by the end of the same year, he makes it to the final table of a tournament and wins about R $ 60,000. The tax on this award will be approximately $ 16,000 and your premium in the year will actually be $ 20,000. This was still a generous example because we can have much worse reflexes by making several possible combinations.

The author, Bachelor of Accounting since 1999, today Professional poker and law student , since he started playing poker re creative in mid-2009, from the beginning sought to develop methods and actions to reduce these tax reflections on his journey, instinct issue Because at first the poker player does not worry about these possible problems, he falls in love with the chance to win dollars and euros.

In chapter 16 you will find the solution to at least reduce the negative tax consequences on your poker profitability.

CONCLUSION

Now, you reader, having read about the subjects that interested you in this book, if you no longer understand what revolves around this magical sport of mind, the game of poker, can now draw your own conclusions on the subject.

I am happy to have covered almost every important concept of poker in this " 2nd Edition of Poker, from leisure to business" and have shown that the application of the game is much larger than previously thought since its application in the academic arena. , in sporting activities, leisure and economic, and may even be a profession for some.

I hope that with the approaches to the book, it is clear that if the game of poker is business opportunity, one should invest in training, discipline, emotional intelligence, and accounting in the pursuit of maximizing profitability.

If you only want poker as a hobby, I recommend that you strictly apply the concept of bank roll management, in this situation, remember that we can all have a definite spending on fun and leisure, so even purely for fun. , apply the concepts of bank roll management (working capital).

If you are academic only, enjoy the intriguing applicability of emotional intelligence in poker and prepare to duel with Artificial Intelligence that will dominate a large part of the job market for years to come.

And finally, if the reader can understand why poker is not really a card game but a people game, it will be reaching the highest possible prize in the game. Congratulations!

THANKS

I cannot help once again starting this thanks to my parents, my wife Soraia and son Daniel for somehow helping me to reach another goal in my career.

I can only thank the opportunity that instrutures of the National Council of Justice, during the Judicial Mediation Course, gave me to give a mini lecture on the subject, a fact that gave me confidence to accelerate this magical project of writing these books. Thank you Dr. Roberto Ferro, Dr. Marilisa Seike and Dr. Célia Passos.

And now, at the launch of the 2nd edition of the book "Poker, from leisure to business", thank my illustrious Prof. Dr Marcelino Sato Matsuda, Coordinator of the Law Course at the Centro Universitário Modulo, (Cruzeiro do Sul University), for the academic knowledge he gave me during the law degree and for the invitation to launch this work at the Institution.

Special thanks to CardPlayer Brasil Magazine for the permission to reproduce some articles and images.

www.litoralpoker.com.br

www.ingramcontent.com/pod-product-compliance
Lightning Source LLC
Chambersburg PA
CBHW070326220526
45467CB00001B/55